Not - Two Is Peace

The World-Friend Adi Da speaks from his island-hermitage, breaking his silence out of his concern for the current plight of humanity. Adi Da invites you to consider his urgent calling for the founding of a Global Cooperative Forum—to address the profound ills of today's world, and to re-establish human civilization based on principles of mutual trust, cooperation, tolerance, prior unity, and the limitless participation of all of humankind in transforming its own destiny.

T he old moral, social, and political "order"
of humankind is now dead.

A new and true and right Way of order of
humankind is, now, and forever hereafter, necessary.

This Free Declaration is the Seed-Utterance of that
new and necessary Way of true and right (and truly
globally, totally, and universally cooperative) order.

World-Friend Adi Da

Not-Two Is Peace

The Ordinary People's Way
of Global Cooperative Order

BY THE WORLD-FRIEND

Adi Da

IS PEACE 723
MIDDLETOWN, CALIFORNIA

International Standard Book Number: 1-57097-214-1
Library of Congress Catalog Card Number: 2006932500

ABOUT THE COVER

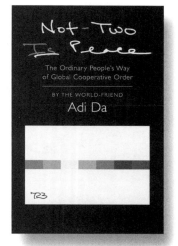

The image on the cover is a flag design created by Adi Da specifically for the Global Cooperative Forum. He explains the significance of the flag as follows:

> National flags represent the already presumed separateness of national identities. In contrast, the Global Cooperative Forum is represented by a single flag, consisting of the simple spectrum of colors on a white field.
>
> The white field is a "tabula rasa" (or blank slate), symbolizing the absence of all the kinds of self-imagery by which human beings create differences between themselves and others. In addition, the plain white flag is a traditional sign of truce or surrender. The party waving the white flag is signalling that it does not want confrontation, and that it is not posing a threat.
>
> The Global Cooperative Forum is not there to confront anyone. It relinquishes all confrontation and all war, and it upholds no self-imagery beyond the simple reality of being part of the totality of humankind.
>
> The presence of the rainbow straight across the flag indicates that the Global Cooperative Forum is actually functioning as a global institution. The spectrum of color on the white field symbolizes inclusiveness in every sense—all flags, all races, and all nations.

The "723" in the lower left corner stands for the date July 23, 2006. In his essay entitled "723" (Part Nine in this book), Adi Da comments on the unique and decisive significance of this date in global human history. ∎

CONTENTS

Not - Two Is Peace

Twelve Laws for World Peace

BY THE WORLD-FRIEND

Adi Da

1. Cooperation + Tolerance = Peace.

2. All of humankind must "lose face" together—in order to require cooperation and tolerance of each other.

3. All war is now genocide. Therefore, armed conflict must no longer be engaged as a means for dealing with world issues.

4. No nation or culture has a right to enact—or even to plan—mass destruction, for any reason whatsoever.

5. The "Humble Unity" of all of humankind is the power that must dissent from all efforts to achieve world domination.

6. The right ordering of human society can only occur on the basis of freedom from any "ruling ideology"—whether that ideology is religious or secular in nature.

7. The universal human rights are <u>unlimited</u> <u>physical</u> <u>participation</u> in the opportunities of human life and <u>unlimited</u> <u>physical</u> <u>protection</u> from harm.

8. The real (even genetic) situation of the human species is <u>prior</u> <u>unity</u>. Peace requires that prior unity be the <u>working-presumption</u> of humankind.

9. The working-presumption of prior unity must become the basis of a global body—or Global Cooperative Forum— that exists to address the urgent global issues that <u>everyone</u> has in common.

10. In that Global Cooperative Forum, all "name-tags" and "slogans" and "flags" must be "left at the door". <u>Every</u> participant would represent <u>all</u> of humankind, as a totality.

11. Ultimately, the habit of presuming to be a separate "self" (confronting a "world-out-there") is to be outgrown in the Enlightened understanding of Reality as inherently One, Non-separate, and Indivisible.

12. <u>Unconditional</u> Peace is the Spiritual Realization of Reality Itself (or Truth Itself)—utterly beyond all presumptions of "separate self" and "world-out-there".

INTRODUCTION

by Carolyn Lee, PhD

When great prophecy is uttered, it is recognized by the wise. Such prophecy is the essence of this book. The essays you are about to read are the "report" of a supremely enlightened sage—telling what he sees, and what must change in order to save human culture and the entire planet from irreversible destruction.

Adi Da speaks as "World-Friend", making his communication out of a profound, intrinsic knowledge of existence, wherein there are no "differences" to be found. As he describes in this book, from the "point of view" of Reality Itself (or That Which <u>Is</u>), the "points of view", the beliefs, the "labels", the self-imagery by which we define ourselves have no ultimate meaning or truth. In other words, he speaks from a position of having transcended all identification with race, or nation, or religion, or any traditional philosophy. Although born in New York (in 1939), Adi Da has established his principal hermitage in Fiji and adopted Fijian citizenship. By thus residing in this small island-nation situated on the international dateline, he is expressing his stance beyond both west and east, and a disposition that is inherently non-political, and full of blessing toward all.

To find a being thus capable of seeing the whole picture of humankind's dilemma, and able to speak to its cure—free of any partisanship, and without any axe to grind—is a truly exceptional boon and grace for this troubled world, wherein all civilizing "authorities", both sacred and secular, have tended to become more and more discredited or disempowered.

While Adi Da characteristically speaks only in the mode of esoteric instruction about the process of ultimate Enlightenment, he speaks here of the most basic realities that are the common concern of all human beings. And his message is that a global shift in the trend of human affairs must begin immediately. In Part Nine of this book, he indicates the mysterious import of "723" (July 23, 2006) as the pivotal date from which humanity's turnabout must start to manifest—in the form of a Global Cooperative Order, led by a Global Cooperative Forum representing all humankind.

Adi Da is simply the wisdom-source of such a forum— not its director. But his wisdom, founded in the inmost knowledge of reality, and of the human heart, is both practical and "radical" (in the sense of "functioning at the root"). He is inviting all human beings to embrace the "723" of life and peace, through cooperation, tolerance, and the transcending of differences, rather than continuing to succumb to the "911" death-mentality of global emergency and end-time conflict.

There has never been greater danger, nor greater opportunity. Humankind cannot afford not to heed the heart-broken warning and inspired calling of its World-Friend, Adi Da, who makes this offering freely to all who can receive it. ■

Not-Two Is Peace

The Ordinary People's Way
of Global Cooperative Order

BY THE WORLD-FRIEND

Adi Da

FIRST WORD

Anthroposphere

(The Natural Zone of Necessary Human Responsibility)

A First Word
About the Unified Global Ecology
of the Necessary New Mode
of Human Civilization

1.

My communication in *Not-Two Is Peace* is a direct address to humankind as a whole, because of the now profoundly changed situation of humankind—a situation that is not really being acknowledged and understood to be the case. In the present time, the social, political, economic, and religious domains of the human sphere are all characterized by a kind of "fundamentalism of the old days", a kind of "retro world"—and this is creating a disaster, because humankind has not shifted in its understanding to account for the real situation that now exists. The current situation is one in which the prior unity of humankind is self-evident—but that prior unity is not being acted upon. Instead, people are still hoisting the old "flags" and looking for "victory".

When human beings were rather independent (or disconnected) from one another and living in tribal groups—isolated by geography, and not so much face-to-face—national States and all kinds of "tribalism" (religious, social, economic, and political) could represent a positive human and ecological influence, each within its own domain. However, in the present time, such "tribalism" can no longer function positively. In the present time, "tribalism" is producing disaster.

National States came into being through the chaotic process of the unfolding of history, in a time when humankind as a whole was not yet interconnected. In that historical situation, the Earth itself, as a natural domain, provided the only "grid" of interconnectedness. The Earth carried on its own natural processes—but, the more human beings became globally connected, the more they interrupted the natural Earth-process. As a result, there are many things happening to the Earth that are the direct result of human intervention. In previous epochs of history, human beings did not intervene in the natural Earth-process to such a degree. Thus, the natural Earth-process, which once held everything together in a kind of order (or unity), is now globally interrupted—along with the entire process of life altogether. Therefore, the Earth is no longer holding things together.

Furthermore, the totality of humankind is now face-to-face. All the different "tribal" arrangements that became national States are playing off one another. Therefore, a new "method" of establishing order is needed, based on the interconnectedness of humankind. There is potential virtue in the fact that all of humankind is now interconnected—but only if humankind can function cooperatively, and in a disposition of tolerance, rather than in the disposition of exclusion and the will-to-dominate.

A rightly functioning and truly all-inclusive Global Cooperative Forum, based upon the working-principle of the prior unity of all of humankind, will make the face-to-face meeting of humankind as a whole into a positive means of political and social order.* Without such a Global Cooperative Forum, there is only going to be more and more "tribal" warfare, creating more and more of a global catastrophe—not only in the historical terms of human disorder, but even in the natural terms of undermining the order of the Earth-process. Indeed, both natural chaos and historical chaos are already happening.

Therefore, there needs to be a new "method" of human politics and social existence, based on the fact that humankind is entirely face-to-face now. All of humankind is interconnected, but that interconnection is tending to be negative—embroiled in (even deliberately generated) conflict, and involved in efforts to expand and control.

There must now be a "method" of establishing order which is based on the interconnectedness of humankind as

---

*Adi Da's full discussion of the principles for such a Global Cooperative Forum is given in Parts Seven, Eight, and Nine of this book.

a whole, and which also assumes responsibility for the right serving of (and for right participation in) the natural order. Only by this means can the disastrous effects of the human exploitation of Earth be brought to an end. There must be a <u>functioning</u> <u>unity</u> of humankind as a whole—dealing with the political, social, and economic order worldwide, as well as with the natural order worldwide.

National States are simply "zones" within this totality— "zones" that should be entirely cooperative. National States are among the kinds of structures (already in place) that have come about through the accidents of history, at a time when humankind was <u>not</u> interconnected as a whole. In the current situation, these inherited structures have become subject to all kinds of power-games and power-struggles all over the world. These structures, in their present form, are not to be merely ignored—but they must become accountable and responsible within a total global order of humankind.

The necessary right and true Global Cooperative Order is not a totalitarian order—that, of course, would not be positive. However, a totalitarian order is exactly what <u>could</u> come about through the disposition of conflict that is now ruling the world, with all the players cloaking themselves in their associations with national States.

In actuality, the situation of humankind has gone through a progressive but dramatic change over the last few centuries—and especially in the last century. Now humankind is <u>already</u> interconnected and <u>already</u> face-to-face. Therefore, the Earth must become a sphere of "priorly united" nations. There must be a Global Cooperative Forum based on prior unity, on principles that have to do with the unified totality of humankind, and the unified totality that is the Earth-domain itself. This is absolutely imperative—because the current disorder and threat to humankind and the Earth is a result of not taking into account the fact that humankind is now an interconnected unity that is face-to-face. That face-to-face situation is currently associated with all kinds of conflict—between different ideologies, different cultural histories, different religious associations, and so forth.

Therefore, as a result of many centuries of change in the human world, an entirely new and different kind of order is required—politically, and (also) environmentally. This is an entirely new situation, that has fully come into being only recently—most especially in the twentieth century (and particularly in the final decades of the twentieth century), and now in the twenty-first century.

The continuation of the "old ways" of doing things, and the persistence in the old habits of mind and life, is producing the current "neighborhood-wars"—as if it were possible to "play it" as in the old days, and expect that, somehow or other, things will work out politically. The "old ways" are no longer applicable. "Tribal" associations—whether religious, national, or racial—no longer have relevance in the now-interconnected state of humankind.

2.

Humankind must wake up. Humanity <u>is</u> now one—and there truly is only <u>one</u> "boat". Everybody <u>is</u> face-to-face <u>now</u>, and the chaotic results of humankind's <u>dis</u>-united and separative (and, altogether, ego-like) activities are, in fact, undermining the natural order on which everybody was able to depend until the last two hundred years, before human intervention started seriously changing the natural Earth-situation itself.

Ego is ruling—but ego has always ruled. The problem is that, now, ego is ruling in a totally different kind of situation, in which ego has the power to destroy not only humankind as a whole, but even the natural order of the Earth-world.

To imagine that a separate absolute Deity is in charge of the current chaos and suffering in the human world and in the Earth-world is to indulge in ignorance. Human beings <u>themselves</u> have intervened. Whatever the origins of the Earth-world are altogether, the natural domain is now being interfered with by human beings, in this time in which humankind has a total effect on the natural world. Therefore, humankind must not merely appeal to a parent-like Deity to change the situation. The "God" That <u>Is</u> Reality Itself expects and requires humankind to change its own act.

Human beings are causing negative events in both the natural world and the political world—because human beings are still mentally indulging in "tribalism", while (in actuality) they are globally face-to-face and in "one boat". The ancient "tribal" mode of human culture—in which human beings live in units that are, effectively, collective forms of egoity, living in conflict with one another—is what must stop.

It is not merely that, suddenly, there are negative happenings in the world. There have always been negative happenings in the world. What is new is that the world is now in a <u>different</u> <u>condition</u> from anything that has existed previously. There is now a <u>new</u> <u>situation</u> for humankind—indeed, a new situation for all of Earthkind, and for the Earth itself. This new condition, wherein humankind exists as a totality in which all are interconnected, must be acknowledged and acted upon.

This new situation requires a profound transformation of human consciousness and human activity. Thus, my communication in *Not-Two Is Peace* is not simply a response to current events, in the sense of the "daily news" of the moment. I am addressing the altogether-new situation that exists for humankind and for the Earth itself—a situation that requires a new kind of politics, a new kind of global human order.

In this new global human order, principles representing the totality of humankind, and the Earth as a whole, must become the means whereby human living is conducted all over the Earth. This will require a kind of global "revolution"—but the root-cause of the "revolution" has already happened. The "revolution" that has already happened is the fact that everybody has already come together, face-to-face, and that the totality of everybody is everywhere affecting the Earth. Therefore, it is imperative that human consciousness catch up, and notice what has happened—and choose what must change.

The terrible problems that are occurring politically and naturally in the world today are the result of pattern-driven human unconsciousness. Human beings are continuing mechanically, trying to repeat modes of effort, even modes of thinking, that were workable—up to a point—in the past, but that are no longer workable now. A new kind of human consciousness is required—based on the working-presumption of prior unity, and on an understanding of the indivisibly single world in which everyone is living. This involves not only the notion that there is such a single world, but it requires grasping the necessity for cooperation, and the necessity to function on the basis of an understanding that the Earth is a single system, and humankind (likewise) is a single whole. Humankind must not be forced to function under some kind of totalitarian singleness. Rather, humankind must function cooperatively—in the sense that everyone is living together on Earth, and functioning through a mechanism of global principles that are benign and right and true.

Not-Two Is Peace is about the new "method" that must be brought to the already existing new global situation. That is the situation to which I have given utterance. The current situation is the result of human unconsciousness, of trying to function automatically on the basis of methods and patterns which applied in the past, but which no longer apply in the present. If the "old" methods are brought to bear in the current situation, they create chaos—human disorder and suffering, as well as chaos in the natural domain.

There is undeniable and inescapable proof in the every day of "daily news" that human beings are <u>everywhere</u> carrying on their activities in a manner that is not productive, and not workable. Humankind must, itself (and as a whole), become truly and rightly globalized. There must be the establishment of principles which serve the potential well-being of humankind as a whole, and which ensure that the Earth-domain itself is able to function soundly. Thus, a different "method" of human relatedness is required: the non-"tribal", or non-fragmented, "method", in which the working-presumption is prior unity.

PART ONE

Humankind Is <u>Literally</u> One Family

There is no difference between people. Human beings are a <u>single</u> species—and, fundamentally, they are all the <u>same</u>. The various colors do not make any difference. Races of human beings are variations of minor genetic changes that developed as human beings wandered the planet and lived under various conditions over thousands of years. Of course, in each place where human beings settled, they developed particular philosophical views and cultural characteristics. Nevertheless, the changes that occurred and the differences that developed are sheerly incidental and minor.

It is important for everyone to understand that <u>humankind</u>, as a species (and as a whole), is (and always has been) characterized by a constant and global process of <u>diaspora</u>. <u>All</u> of humankind is wandering all over the Earth. Humankind (and even life itself, as a singular whole) is, historically and characteristically, <u>dispersed</u> (or scattered). However, in its fragmentation (as many and separate everythings), human-kind is, now, acting as if it is not <u>one</u> thing, but, rather, as if it were many different and separate somethings—as if tribal differentiation into national, and religious, and cultural particularity, and distinct racial groupings, and distinct language types, and so forth, amounts to a fundamental difference-making force that should redefine humankind, not as one indivisible species, but as many separate and competing species.

<u>All</u> of the apparent diversity of humankind is a superficial diversity within the context of a <u>single</u> (and <u>inherently indivisible</u>) species—which, according to the best (even genetic) analysis, progressively moved out of Africa and into various parts of the world. Therefore, now, the indivisible totality of humankind is dispersed—with relatively small groupings of people having, in times past, become stationary in one or another geographical (and, now, also cultural) location, and (thus and thereby) having become attached to

their unique local languages and political systems and religious traditions, and on and on and on and on. There is no end to the local (or "tribal") differences—and human beings tend to make much of the apparent differences between them. However, the apparent differences are (in Truth) merely superficial (or local, and, thus, "tribal", or merely provincial) characteristics—the ordinary variants on what it is to be a human being, located in "point of view" relative to space and time.

The negative (and competitive) presumption of "difference" in the context of the universal human diaspora is a problem of fundamental significance—and it is a problem (or a presumption) that must now come to an end. There must be a presumed prior unity (or inherent indivisibility) of humankind—not the domination over all others by one nation (or "type"), and not some numbers of nations (or "similars") indulging in strategic conflict with one another, in order to wage a "final battle" to determine who is going to dominate and rule everybody else.

It is as if all human beings suddenly do not recognize their own brothers and sisters. It is true that one may look different from another, and one may carry a different cultural inheritance and mode of thinking than another, and so on. Therefore, human beings may all look and think differently—but they all are and do the same thing. Everyone must become educated to notice this.

Human beings are all primates—not exactly apes, but something along those lines. How much knowledge do you think a primate inherently possesses? Why would you expect a totally rightly informed mind to be demonstrated by a casually adapted primate?

Why do you—the people of humankind—continue to insist on making the differences that you make, on the basis of local historical memories and provincial institutional configurations of separate groups of people? Why do you do that, instead of understanding that what you are observing, right now, is the indivisible global singleness of a particular species? Every human being is, <u>as such</u>, always already coincident with (and fundamentally identical to) every other—and, therefore, could also be combined, in a very productive and positive sense, with the total world of all of humankind. What is required is the establishing of a Global Cooperative (and universally participatory) Order of humankind—a cultural and social and political globalization of humankind (and not merely an economic globalization of human commerce, within a world-situation characterized by <u>competitive differences</u>).

The diaspora of <u>all</u> of humankind must be reacculturated, to accept and embrace a universal "homeland of everywhere". The total world of human beings must grow up, to understand humankind as an indivisible totality, now everywhere dispersed, not merely by contemporary political forces, but by the migration of the human species all over the globe for countless thousands of years, and by the accumulation of localized characteristics of life and mind under all kinds of different local (and geographically separate) conditions.

Humankind is in the position, right now, to make some very important judgements about life, and about the relationships between people—and about Reality Itself. As a result of that judgement, either there will be universal war and death or, alternatively, humankind will become established in a Global Cooperative Order, based on the working-presumption of universal prior unity and the universal world-"homeland" that belongs to <u>all</u> of humankind (and, indeed, <u>all</u> of Earthkind).

<u>All</u> have suffered. <u>All</u> are equally full of nonsense. Therefore, in principle, there must be a new and universal politics—a politics of <u>no</u> praise and <u>no</u> blame. By these means, reconciliation must be achieved—cooperatively, in a disposition of mutual tolerance, trust, and respect.

The genetic unity of humankind is <u>inherent</u>. That unity is scientifically known to be <u>so</u>. Yet, the "difference-makers" speak and act as if there were superior humans and inferior humans, superior nationalisms and inferior nationalisms, and so on—as if merely incidental differences were of immense significance. To make much of incidental differences is merely to argue about old stories. Instead of all that, everyone must be exercised anew—toward (and in, and <u>As</u>) Truth in always present-time.

PART TWO

C + T = P:
Formula for World Peace

1.

I t is a matter of the <u>greatest</u> present-time urgency that the prevailing global mood of political separatism, end-game competitiveness, and endlessly multiplied divisiveness be immediately and thoroughly and universally and permanently relinquished—such that the entire world-population of humankind becomes universally intelligent with the heart-positive mind of cooperation and tolerance.

2.

The only way to solve the current world-situation is for <u>everyone</u> to "<u>lose</u> face"—instead of everyone demanding to "<u>save</u> face".

All of humankind should, as a formalized collective, "lose face" together—by acknowledging that, unless human beings live in formally established and formally maintained cooperation and tolerance, they, <u>inevitably</u>, sink into grossly and universally destructive behavior.

Only by <u>everyone</u> "losing face" <u>together</u> will the collective of human beings be able to regenerate the moral strength and authority that is necessary if human beings everywhere are to require cooperation and tolerance of each other—and only when there is <u>first</u> such a regeneration of universally equalized moral strength and authority will there be a universal agreement to create and maintain a truly cooperative and tolerant global human community.

3.

Human beings must accept, with humility, that their rightful position (and that of every one) in the naturally indivisible world-family of Earthkind (including humankind) is not the "ego-place" of <u>prior dis-unity</u> (and, thus, of separateness, separativeness, domination, and control), but the "heart-place" of <u>prior</u> <u>unity</u> (and, thus, of ego-transcending cooperation and tolerance).

It is not the <u>search</u> for peace (for <u>all</u> seeking is, necessarily, based on prior, or presumed, separation from what is being sought), but the <u>active</u> <u>affirmation</u> and <u>enactment</u> of peace (or the presumption of prior, or always already present, unity and non-conflict—as a condition to be <u>always</u> affirmed, depended upon, enacted, and preserved) that is the true and only means for the realization of peace.

Thus, in practical terms, it is <u>only</u> on the active foundation of ego-transcending cooperation and tolerance that it is possible for peace (or right life) to be established among living beings of <u>any</u> form or kind.

Indeed, this Call to Right Life and Peace is a great and absolute moral Law, which I have Epitomized in the Formula C + T = P, or "Cooperation + Tolerance = Peace".

It is absolutely essential that the universal collective of humankind formally embrace and really enact this universal moral disposition.

4.

"Cooperation + Tolerance = Peace" is the Great Alternative to the egoic path of inevitable universal destruction—and, therefore, that moral Law must become a universally accepted (<u>and</u> expected) moral and practical self-discipline.

Through the universal application of this great moral Law, the gathering of the Earth-wandering peoples of the world can feel their real strength and prior unity (or inherent connectedness to one another)—and their collective power to transform the "usual" (or "real") politics of egoity, and so actually create and maintain human peace in the natural world.

Everyone should become positively disposed to the establishment of a real and true global cooperative human community—because that global cooperative human community is not merely a "utopian ideal", but a practical and actually realizable necessity for the physical survival and the natural well-being of humankind and even all of Earthkind.

5.

The Formula for World Peace must be embraced as the necessary politics of the future.

Cooperation and tolerance is the necessary and exact "price" for peace—the "treaty cost" for the survival of humankind, Earthkind, and Earth itself.

This is the necessary "new paradigm" for the human design of future effort.

PART THREE

On Liberation from ego
<u>and</u> egoic Society

1.

The un-En-Light-ened (or egocentric) body-mind-self is founded on the activity of self-contraction. The self-contraction is expressed as the effective differentiation of the presumed "self" from the Transcendental, Inherently Spiritual, Inherently egoless, and Self-Evidently Divine (or Acausally Real) Self-Condition and Source-Condition, and from every other form of presumed (or, by means of self-contraction, defined) "not-self". And the self-contraction is, likewise, expressed (via the self-contraction-definition of "self" as independent and separative) as the constant concern and search for the preservation of the (presumed-to-be independent) "self" (or ego-"I"). The self-based (or self-contracting, and would-be-self-preserving) orientation toward existence is manifested as the psychology of search and conflict relative to all that is presumed to be "not-self"—some and all of which is sometimes desired and sought, and some and all of which is sometimes feared (or reacted to with the seeking effort of avoidance), and even all of which is <u>always</u> limited, mortal, passing, inexplicable, and (therefore) inherently unsatisfactory. Therefore, the psychology of self-contracted (and, as a result, egocentric) existence is inherently disposed to seek control and dominance over all that is presumed to be "not-self". For this reason, individual egocentric lives are a constant expression of heart-felt (and total psycho-physical) anxiety (and even the primitive ego-moods of fear, sorrow, anger, and every kind of un-love)—and individual human actions are, on that primitive basis, always a more or less mechanical (or uninspected and irresponsible) display of strategic techniques of self-manipulation (intended to preserve "self") and other-manipulation (intended to control, or dominate, "not-self"). And the collective (or group) life of egocentric human beings is, likewise, dominated by the same exclusiveness, the same emotional base, the same inherent unsatisfactori-ness, and the same motives toward self-preservation, and toward control of what is "outside".

Human societies are always tending to be modeled after the un-En-Light-ened pattern of the individual ego. The political and social systems of the present-day world are not generated by literally En-Light-ened (or even highly "evolved") leaders, ideals, or institutions. Human beings in this "late-time" (or "dark" epoch) live in the un-En-Light-ened world of egoic society—and this is why the signs of the times are so profoundly negative.

The entire world is now nearly out of control with egoic motives. Humankind, indoctrinated by materialistic philoso-phies, ego-serving technologies, and gross political idealisms, is possessed by the mechanical and emotionally negative efforts of self-indulgence (and anxious release-seeking efforts of all kinds), and chronically depressed by the frustration of the Transcendental Spiritual impulses that are the inherent characteristics of the heart of every living being. The ego-"I", whether individual or collective, is eventually reduced to sorrow and despair (or chronic life-depression), because of (and as an experiential result of) the inability of life (in and of itself) to generate Happiness and Joy and Immortality. And that self-contained depression finally becomes anger, or loveless confrontation with the total world and every form of presumed "not-self"—including even (and especially) the Transcendental, Inherently Spiritual, Inherently egoless, and Self-Evidently Divine (or Acausally Real) Self-Identity (or One and Only and Non-Separate Self-Condition), Which is "locked away", by means of conventional (or merely exo-teric) ideas of "God Apart", and is (thereby) made into an "Other" by the egoic mind. And, when anger becomes the mood of human societies, the quality of fire (or the primitive and destructive intent of the frustrated ego) invades the plane of humanity. That fire is expressed as all of the aggression and competitiveness (and all of the resultant suf-ferings and painful illusions) of humankind, including all of the ego-based politics of confrontation. And that ego-fire is, finally, summarized in the acts of war.

2.

The differentiation of existence into ego-possessed units yields, in the case of each "one", the craving for entirely pleasurized and unthreatened existence. This craving (or obsessive motive of self-preservation and self-glorification) in turn yields inevitable conflict, fear, sorrow, anger, and all kinds of destructive acts in relation to "others" as well as to "self" (because the extreme exercise of self-preservation is, ultimately, an aggressive and self-defeating motivation that destroys "self" in the final effort to dominate "not-self"). Therefore, all egos (or un-En-Light-ened centers of identity, whether individual or collective) are in aggressive conflict with all other egos (and all that is presumed to be "not-self", or presumed to be "outside" the defined egoic center). All individual and collective egos are involved in programs of self-destruction (via patterns of ego-possession, self-seeking, self-indulgence, reactive emotion, un-En-Light-ened thinking, and so forth), as well as other-destruction (via all kinds of reactive activity, based on self-concern, that seeks to control, and, ultimately, to dominate, whatever is presumed to be "outside" the "self"-center).

The search for the independent preservation and ultimate enhancement of the separate self is the universal model of un-En-Light-ened egoity. Therefore, suffering, power struggle, and war are inevitable in egoic society. And, if the capability for political manipulation and war becomes technologically profound, universal suppression (via aggressive political efforts) and universal destruction (via war) become the common expectation and destiny of all human beings.

The present "late-time" (or "dark" epoch) is just such a time of technological sophistication, in which the egoic model of humanity and human society is the universal basis of mind. Gross materialism (in science and politics) gives human beings no option in the mind except that of the trapped and threatened animal. Therefore, a fiery mood is abroad—full of gross desire, frustration, fear, despair, and aggressive reactivity. The egoic motive of self-preservation is approaching its most destructive mood—the mood that appears in the moment of ultimate entrapment. In that mood, there is no longer any will to preserve "self" or world or any others. There is simply explosive fire—based on the deep motives of egoic self-preservation, but reduced to action that is most primitive and entirely destructive of both "self" and "not-self". In the collective mind of humanity in the present and growing extremes of entrapment, the explosion of great nuclear bombs merely represents the archetype of anger itself. And it is for this reason that the possibility of a nuclear holocaust, in the extreme moment of the now rising political confrontations, is an irrational—and, therefore, entirely possible, if not inevitable—event.

Past societies have, in their extreme moments of confrontation, destroyed themselves, as well as their opponents. This is because ego-based societies function in essentially the same manner as egoic individuals. Individual human beings kill others and themselves every day. Therefore, groups and societies, confronting one another in egoic fashion, likewise threaten one another with destruction. And, in the extreme moments of confrontation, when self-preservation achieves its peak of righteous irrationality, it is profoundly likely that nuclear war will result.

The motives of present-day society are the same as those of past societies. The only difference is that, in the present day, the technology of both communication and confrontation has become both globally extended and profound. Therefore, when globally communicated confrontation reaches its peak of irrationality, war-motives will willingly destroy the entire world—just as readily as, in the past, less technologically sophisticated war-makers have wiped their petty local warring tribes from the face of the Earth.

3.

Many people are now trying to influence govern-ments to abandon nuclear weapons. However, even if they succeed, irrational individuals and groups can still threaten and destroy the common order with "ter-rorist" tactics and "home-made" bombs. And the "limited" (or non-nuclear) warfare that might still erupt between gov-ernments that agree not to make nuclear war is just as much a threat to humanity as any nuclear war.

Therefore, it is <u>now</u> time to accept the political necessity for an end to confrontation-politics, and the establishment of a unified political entity to directly and truly and formally and accountably serve the right collective interests of humankind as a whole. Human beings must abandon their ancient egoic principles and renounce their political, social, and cultural provincialism. <u>Individuals</u> within the collective order of humankind may yet suffer the un-En-Light-ened and immature disabilities of egocentric personality—but <u>governments</u> themselves, as well as institutions and leaders in every area of human endeavor, must abandon the ego-centric, subhuman, merely materialistic, non-cooperative, and intolerant (or loveless) posture and style of life. Indeed, humanity as a whole must demand that a new leadership of this kind come forward and accept responsibility, in a uni-fied (and truly representative and accountable) manner, for the indivisible representation of its collective interests.

Have <u>you</u> not had enough of the brute, stupid, childish, and (otherwise) adolescent, exploitative representation of human (or, really, sub-human) existence that is played out daily (in the name, and on the lives, of each and every born human being) by competing governments, politicians, mili-tarists, scientists, technocrats, social planners, educators, exoteric and fundamentalist religionists (who aggressively propagate the provincial religions of ego-<u>salvation</u>, rather than practice the universal, and ego-<u>transcending</u>, religion of love), and media hypers (who thrive on the invention and exaggeration of conflict, and dramatically showcase the worst of human instincts in the unending "gotcha" game that denudes and exposes and trivializes and hypocritically mocks the highs, and the inevitable lows, and even the natural ordinariness in the struggling efforts of humankind)? Is it not evident, in your deepest feeling-psyche, that this Wisdom-renouncing world is now being controlled by the worst and most superficial conceptions of existence?

It is <u>now</u> time for every one, and all, to understand themselves, and to reclaim the world from the dictatorship of the ego, and from all of those who play at politics (and life in general) as if it were a TV sporting event that is supposed to excite and entertain everyone.

Nuclear disarmament is a relatively positive, but still too superficial and piecemeal, effort. It is not a truly curative means, but only another palliative and temporary move in the midst of humankind's traditional advance toward future trouble. There is something more fundamental than the disarmament politics whereby <u>enemies</u> come to a gentlemanly agreement on how to kill one another without destroying one another! What is more fundamental, necessary, and truly curative is that human beings, individually and collectively, understand and transcend that which is in them that leads them to confront one another as opponents and enemies.

It may sound naive to speak of the necessity for the childish and brutishly adolescent governments and institutions to understand themselves and renounce the self-imagery and the techniques of enemies—but the feeling that it is naive to speak in such terms is merely a reflection of egoic frustration and despair. Human beings everywhere must <u>now</u> transcend that very frustration and despair if they are going to prevent the enslavement and destruction of humankind.

Humanity is living in bondage <u>now</u>. Humankind is already—<u>presently</u>, globally—bound to egocentric and materialistic idealisms that are suppressing the human freedom to live by Wisdom and Realize the Truth. If human beings do not shake loose from this regime, they are going to suffer the extreme fulfillment of collective egoic destiny, in a "Narcissistic" holocaust that will either enslave humankind (via a technologically robotized political and social order) or (otherwise) destroy humankind (via technologically engineered warfare).

It is <u>not</u> naive to demand a new leadership when those who are led (and who <u>could</u> make the counter-demand for change) number in the billions. Nor is it folly to try to educate humankind when the only alternative is slavery and death. Therefore, <u>all</u> must commit themselves to understand the patterns by which they are now (and have traditionally and historically been) living (both individually and collectively), so that they can then change those patterns and the destinies those patterns will (otherwise) inevitably inflict upon them.

The egoic model must—from <u>now</u> on—be <u>intensively</u> "educated out" of the collective order of humankind. A new leadership must <u>now</u> appear, which is awakened to an understanding of the primitive egoic basis of the present and traditional collective order. That new leadership must, above all, provide an <u>educative</u> role—and it must, profoundly and immediately, transform the techniques whereby governments and societies enter into relations with one another. Only such leadership can, by efforts based on the wit of free intelligence, cause all the governments and institutions of the world to voluntarily change toward a cooperative and benign mode of association with others. If this kind of approach is not made soon, humanity will be entering into what has the potential to be the most destructive period of political confrontation in its history.

4.

A benign and tolerant and cooperative (or non-egoic, and at least more advanced, if not Transcendentally Spiritual) view of existence (and, thus, of politics) must now arise in the leadership of humankind. At the present time, human beings are being led to enslavement and destruction by benighted materialists and self-seekers in every area of common human endeavor. The Principle of Wisdom has been replaced by the principle of power-through-knowledge—and knowledge has come to mean the views and presumed knowledge determined by the culture and method of scientific materialism, or all that can be achieved or supported exclusively by the intellectual efforts of materialistic philosophy. Science (which has characteristi-cally identified itself with the archaic and false philosophy of materialism) has itself, thus, become identical to technology (or the materialistic power-machine of the "known"), and materialistic technology (along with its like in the form of all the materialistic idealisms that appeal to human egoity) has become the primary instrument for world-manipulation—not only for the material manipulation of the so-called "material" world, but for the political manipulation and gross (physical and mental) control of collective humanity itself.

The political ideals and means of the present time are materialistic, based on a gross and ego-based conception of human existence. There simply cannot be any ultimately effective change in the collective human situation until a new leadership arises that is founded on the intelligence and more advanced capability of ego-transcendence and, ulti-mately, on the Wisdom of Transcendental, Inherently Spiritual, Inherently egoless, and Self-Evidently Divine (or Acausally Real) En-Light-enment. Only such a leadership can rightly educate the collective order and relieve it of the burden of the egoic and materially confined view of life.

And only such a leadership can transform the technique of governments from a process of self-preserving and other-controlling confrontation (of their own members, as well as other societies) to a process of cooperation, unification, and a worldwide creative order, based (necessarily) on pluralism, tolerance, and freedom.

The problem of the automatic (and even unconscious) creation of suffering and destruction is inherent in the ego-centric form of individual existence. It is this principle that all must observe and understand in themselves. Human beings must learn from this observation of the ego (in both personal and collective terms), and so equip themselves to freely (both personally and collectively) abandon the egoic model of existence.

5.

The life-principles of abandoning the gross style of ego-based political confrontations and ego-based social participation, or non-participation, must become a matter of active practical commitment on the part of the leaders and educators of humankind—or else humanity will collectively move toward intolerable enslavement and even nuclear (or otherwise war-made, and cleverness-made) destruction.

Therefore, every one and all must consider, and, then, actively embrace every form of true and benign social and political cooperation and all-embracing social and political tolerance—since such cooperation and tolerance are the prerequisites for true social and political peace.

All the leaders and educators of humankind (now, and forever hereafter) must actively embrace, and universally declare and promote, and actively require and measure the universal real fulfillment of the simplest Law and Measure of right human life: Cooperation + Tolerance = Peace.

PART FOUR

The Three Great Principles
Of All Truth

I. The Divine Principle of Indivisibility: Reality (Itself) is <u>Inherently</u> Indivisible (One and Divine and Non-conditional and Absolute)

II. The Universal (or Cosmic) Principle of Unity and Non-"Difference": The world (or the conditionally manifested cosmos) is <u>Inherently</u> a Unity (Which, in and <u>As</u> its True Self-Condition, is <u>Inherently</u> Non-"different" from the One and Indivisible and Absolute and Non-conditional Divine Reality)

III. The psycho-physical Principle of Non-Separateness: The individual psycho-physical entity is <u>Inherently</u> Non-separate from the world-Unity (or the Inherently Unified cosmic Totality, Which is Whole and Universal) and, also, <u>Inherently</u> Non-separate from the Inherently Indivisible Divine Reality (or the One and Conscious Light That <u>Is</u> the One and Only Self-Condition of all-and-All)

These Three Principles, Proposed by me, are (Effectively) an Integrated Whole and Single Proposition. They (Together) Comprise the Right and True Basis (and the Right and True Measure) for the Correct (and, inevitably, intellectually Liberating) Evaluation of <u>any</u> and <u>all</u> possible propositions of philosophical import made (now, or in the future, or in any time and place at all) by any one (or any school or tradition) at all.

PART FIVE

The Time-Tested Politics of Unity and the Anti-Civilization Politics of Individuation

Politics, society, and the common behavioral norms of any collective order are modeled in the likeness of the concept (or philosophy) of conditionally manifested reality that characterizes the collective generally.

If the prevailing concept (or philosophy) of conditionally manifested reality espouses the presumption that conditionally manifested existence is not a unity (but, instead, is characterized by irreducible multiplicity, separateness, independent individuality, and polar opposition), then the collective order will be characterized by the gross politics of dissociative individuation, and by the universally socially-active idea of competitive individualism, and, also, by behavioral norms and expectations that exclusively correspond to the purpose of separate and separative individual self-fulfillment.

If, however, the prevailing concept (or philosophy) of conditionally manifested reality espouses the presumption that conditionally manifested existence is priorly (or inherently) a unity (and is, for that reason, altogether characterized by, and to be conformed to, the sign of indivisible unity), then the collective order will be characterized by the politics of cooperative unity, and by the universally socially-active idea of social indivisibility, and, also, by self-subordinating behavioral norms and expectations—including such norms as cooperation, tolerance, and globally universal peace.

The traditional, time-tested, and life-proven concept (or philosophy) of conditionally manifested reality is that of <u>prior unity</u>. Politics, society, and the culture of human behavior have traditionally been developed on the basis of the fundamental working-presumption of the prior (or inherent) unity of conditionally manifested reality and the Prior (or Inherent) Oneness (and Indivisibility) of the Non-conditional Reality (or the Source-Condition That <u>Is</u> Reality Itself). And this fundamental presumption, first confessed and communicated by men and women of great Spiritual development, has been the very basis for the universal efforts and purposes of humankind that characterize what is rightly called "civiliza-tion". By contrast—except for the basic corrective demand that appropriate individual rights, and true individual well-being, and necessary individual integrity be properly respected and served—the political, social, and general behavioral signs and results of the concept (or philosophy) of conditionally manifested reality as a non-unity (or an objective multiplicity divorced from Prior Indivisibility) can largely be described as the effort and purpose of counter-civilization, or anti-civilization, or even barbarism. That is to say, the political, social, and general behavioral signs and results of the concept (or philosophy) of conditionally man-ifested reality as a non-unity (or a realm of mere multiplicity, separateness, independent individuality, and polar opposi-tion) are those of ego-glorification, general dissociativeness and separativeness, collective disunity and disorder, indis-criminate exploitation of all possibilities, abuse and disregard of every form of authority, the magnification of every kind of conflict and difference, the exaggeration of competitiveness, self-indulgence, and the purpose of material acquisition, the breakdown of community and collective culture, the devalu-ation and the waning of true philosophical and Spiritual endeavor, and the undermining of the fundamental morality of cooperation, tolerance, and general peacefulness.

Political, social, and general behavioral "materialism" (or conventional "realism") are bound to the concept (or philos-ophy) of conditionally manifested existence as a non-unity (and, at best, a search for the achievement of unity). And such political, social, and general behavioral "materialism" (or conventional "realism") is the overriding common pat-tern and motion of present-time global pseudo-civilization (in spite of the always continuing propaganda that merely idealizes and gives lip service to political and social "unity").

Global peace, human freedom, and human well-being for all of humankind depend on an individual and a collective change of mind—followed by a corresponding change of action. It is a matter of converting the mind and the life and the entire human collective to a right understanding of conditionally manifested reality (which is, inherently, a great unity), and to a right (and truly Spiritual) surrender to the Non-conditional Source-Reality (Which <u>Is</u>, Inherently, One and Indivisible).

When the way of living becomes the active surrender of egoity, then the conditions of life will constantly prove the Truth.

PART SIX

Prior Unity
Rules No Kingdom Here

The Totalitarian Politics of
"Revelation" and "Rulership"
Must Be Transcended and Avoided—
By Means of the Global Exercise of
the Principles of Right and True Civilization

The three principal religious traditions of the Middle East are Judaism, Christianity, and Islam.

Each of the three traditions is a variant on the religious mode of thinking called "monotheism" (which conceives of the world and the human being with reference to a "God"-idea that defines Ultimate Reality as being both One and Indivisible).

In their origins, all three traditions have the same general Semitic cultural, social, and political background—except that Christianity, uniquely among the three, was immediately and coincidently developed (and extended to outside and beyond the general Semitic domain of politics, society, and culture) by means of a thorough re-acculturation (and a thorough social and political re-adaptation) to the cultural, social, and political domain of ancient Greece and Rome.

All three of these monotheistic traditions are, in their "official" formulations, thoroughly exoteric (or public-oriented) in their nature and context—and each of them has always tended toward the status of an "official" State-religion.

All three of these traditions are composed of three principal elements: the "Book", the "Teacher", and the "Religion".

In Judaism, the "Book" is the "Torah" (or the "Five Books of Moses")—and the "Hebrew Bible" as a whole is the larger text of the essential tradition.

In Christianity, the "Book" is the "New Testament" (and, especially, the "Four Gospels").

In Islam, the "Book" is the "Koran".

In Judaism, the "Teacher" is Moses (the "Law-Giver").

In Christianity, the "Teacher" is Jesus (the "Savior", or the "Christ").

In Islam, the "Teacher" is Mohammed (the "Prophet").

In Judaism, the "Religion" is the "Temple"-cult of Jerusalem (the ancient priestly "Seat of the original Kingdom").

In Christianity, the "Religion" is the cult of the "Eucharist" (both as the ritual of the perpetual "Sacrifice" of Jesus as the

"Savior-Christ" <u>and</u> the ritual of the perpetual re-"Ascension" of Jesus to the "Throne" of cosmic "Kingship" as the "Son of God").

In Islam, the "Religion" is the cult of the "Doctrines and Traditions" (of Mohammed, the "Revealer of the Book").

There are numerous particular historical, cultural, doctrinal, and cultic differences between these three monotheistic traditions, but the principal difference between each of them (in comparison to the other two) is in relation to the doctrinal idea of what constitutes the principal (or characteristic and unique) "Revelation" that is the core of the particular tradition.

In Judaism, the "Book" is the "Revelation".

In Christianity, the "Teacher" is the "Revelation".

In Islam, the "Religion" is the "Revelation".

For Judaism, the "Book" (or the "Divine Words") must achieve the "Final Victory" (whereby, at the "end of time", the politically-established priestly tradition of Judaism will "Rule the world").

For Christianity, the "Teacher" (or the "Incarnation of the Divine Word") must achieve the "Final Victory" (whereby, at the "end of time", the politically-established sacramental tradition of Christianity will "Rule the world").

For Islam, the "Religion" (or the politically-established religious movement "Inspired by the Divine Word") must achieve the "Final Victory" (whereby, at the "end of time", the authoritarian religio-political tradition of Islam will "Rule the world").

Fundamentally, among all the religious traditions of the world, <u>only</u> Judaism, Christianity, and Islam are inherently (and aggressively) associated with an expansionistic ideal (and an attitude of not only cultural, but also social and political, superiority) that irreducibly intends (and actively pursues) the self-appointed destiny of total world-domination (or global totalitarian "Rulership").

Likewise, by their very nature, these three religious (and comprehensively and irreducibly cultural, social, <u>and</u> political) traditions are, perpetually, in an intentionally performed state of competition, that always seeks (and frequently achieves) conflict, confrontation, and even aggressive warfare with one another—and even with all other religious, cultural, social, and political traditions, systems, or institutions in the world.

Because of all of this, humankind as a whole must especially beware of these three religious, cultural, social, and political traditions (including all of their variant formulations, systems, and institutions).

Likewise, humankind as a whole must, by all right cooperative means, refuse to allow (and, altogether, act to prevent) these three traditions—and, indeed, any and all other traditions, systems, or institutions—from achieving any kind of larger public state of conflict, confrontation, or otherwise aggressive (or even war-like) opposition either to one another or to any of the other religious, cultural, social, and/or political traditions, systems, or institutions in the public world.

The total world of humankind can easily be drawn into a terminal state of conflict by means of the public theatrical exploitation of the mummer's false-face of exoteric "religion"—only, in due course, to find that a "dark" political, social, and cultural tyranny has been embraced by seemingly "lightest" means.

The world of humankind as a whole must, now, and forever hereafter, embrace and maintain a new, true, and (because of the now global mutuality of humankind as a whole) unique integrity of civilization wherein and whereby <u>all</u> religious, cultural, social, and political traditions, systems, and institutions are perpetually disciplined (and, thus and thereby, kept in balance) by means of the civilizing global exercise of the principles of totality, universality, prior unity, tolerance, and cooperation.

If there is a lapse or a failure in that self-disciplining integrity on the part of the universal totality of humankind, then religious, cultural, social, and/or political factions can (and will) arise in the midst, and even become everywhere (and in a totalitarian manner) dominant, by exploiting the divisions, and the weaknesses, and the ignorance of the otherwise separate parts of the human world.

Therefore, the now necessary global civilization of the totality of humankind requires the self-discipline that is the universal, and comprehensive, and all-including exercise of holistic integrity—or the everywhere exercise of the principle of prior unity, demonstrated by means of mutual cooperation and mutual tolerance (and, thus and thereby, the self-enforcement of a global state of peace)—and this rather than the totalitarian achievement and authoritarian enforcement of universal global "Rulership" on the part of any separately particularized idealism (whether religious, cultural, social, or political in its nature).

By means of the universal global exercise of active true civilization by the "all" of humankind together, all totalitarian idealisms—whether religious, cultural, social, or political in their nature—must be required to renounce and relinquish their presumptions of superiority and their programs of global domination.

However, if humankind as a whole does not establish and embrace a truly civilized Global Cooperative Order (and a globally effective Global Cooperative Forum), all those who imagine they have the exoteric "Rights" of ego-based exclusive "Revelation" (whether religious, cultural, social, or political) will never cease (by every kind of exercise of "Power" and "War") to pursue authoritarian and totalitarian world-domination by means of the final establishing of "Kingdom" and "Rule" by their own "Winning Side".

The "Powers" of national States that would exercise themselves in the name of one or the other of the three "Great Religions" of the Middle East now presume they can wage "Final War" and, thus and thereby, establish "Final

Rule"—and they are now actively moving themselves on that basis.

There is only one human "Power" on Earth that can restore the "Balance of Power" and prevent the global conflagration now planned by the "Mummers of Religion".

That "Power" that must now Dissent, and Nay the course of all the "Holy Plans", is the "Humble Unity" of the <u>all</u> of humankind <u>As</u> <u>One</u>.

PART SEVEN

You The People

On The Necessity
of
A Global Cooperative Order
of
The <u>All</u> of Humankind

1.

The working-presumption of <u>prior</u> unity—rather than the <u>search</u> for unity—is the right and true context for all human exchanges. If there is the working-presumption of prior unity, then ego-surrendering cooperation and tolerance make perpetual human peace. If there is no working-presumption of <u>prior</u> <u>unity</u>, then human interactions become a mere game of competitive egos. And that competitive game is, now, on the verge of destroying humankind and the Earth itself—even at every level of ordinary, and natural, and economic, and political, and, altogether, social life. That competitive and, at last, constantly confrontational ego-game is a struggle that inevitably occurs in every context of presumed <u>non</u>-unity and separateness— thus producing a situation in which <u>everybody</u> is trying to dominate <u>everybody</u> else. That relentlessly competitive and confrontational situation is a lunatic-asylum game that, ultimately, threatens the very survival of life on Earth.

The entire world is now on the verge of absolute destruction—and for no necessary or justifiable reason whatsoever. The Measure of Truth is not being brought to bear on this situation. Therefore, there is, apparently, no readily applicable means for controlling the madness. It appears there are only competing crowds of factionalists, each crowd advocating its local "absolute"—in political or religious or whatever terms. Nothing—no Truth or Greater Reality—is presumed to be senior to the local beliefs, claims, and demands of every tribe of "Everyman".

In order to function rightly and effectively, any human collective—and, therefore, even the collective totality of <u>all</u> the nations of the world—must be based on the working-presumption of <u>prior</u> <u>unity</u> (or <u>inherent</u> <u>indivisibility</u>). At this moment in history, there is <u>nothing</u> "united" about the nations of the world. They are, presently, <u>entirely</u> dis-united, divided, competitive, and confrontational—and entirely possessed by the rage of difference.

People commonly presume unity to be a positive value. But they are typically thinking of unity as something to be "worked toward". "Working toward" unity is not what I am talking about. I am talking about prior unity. I am talking about people entering into a dialogue that is based on the working-presumption of prior unity, and non-separateness, and zero-confrontation, and global indivisibility, and the absolute Law of unbreakable peace—rather than a status quo based on the ego-based presumption of separateness, and conflict, and competition.

A certain benign energy can be associated with competition—when that competition is "in its right place" within human society. But, when the world itself becomes a competition, then competition is no longer in its right place.

What is senior to competition is prior unity (or inherent indivisibility). As a working-principle applicable to all modes of dialogue and all modes of happening in the world, the working-presumption of prior unity is essential. That is why cooperation and tolerance are not merely "ideals"—which people should "try to make happen". Rather, true cooperation and true tolerance originate from the working-presumption of prior unity. Therefore, it is not that you should seek unity, or seek cooperation, or seek tolerance, or seek peace. Unity, cooperation, tolerance, and peace are the Law and the inevitable demonstration of right life. Unity, cooperation, tolerance, and peace are what always already is. Therefore, unity, cooperation, tolerance, and peace must always be presumed to be the principle that is also presently the case—and, then, human beings must always function on the basis of that always present-time working-presumption.

The very opposite of the Law of right life is now presumed in the usual and common dialogues within the human world. Words like "unity" and "cooperation" and "tolerance" and "peace" are used, but they are typically used in the egoic sense—not in the right sense, of being <u>priorly</u> the case, but in the egoic sense, of being something to seek, or something to affirm idealistically, as a technique of propaganda for manipulating people and situations.

There needs to be a fundamental right dialogue functioning in the human world. And that dialogue needs to have a globally-extended and <u>all</u>-representing and <u>all</u>-participating institutional setting, in order to give it form—but that right globally-extended institution will be made to happen only if humankind ceases to be corrupted by the presumption of non-unity (or the presumption that prior unity, or inherent indivisibility, is not <u>always</u> <u>already</u> the case).

2.

The human world has become a kind of insane sporting event, at which people threaten one another and carry on in an insane manner—something like the gladiatorial contests in ancient Rome. It is madness. And TV also plays to that insanity. Everywhere, people and groups look to get attention by getting themselves on TV—often through the exercise of rotten and demented violence, and through the exercise of an altogether aggravated disposition. The human world of nowtime is a lunatic asylum, a soap opera of mummers. That absurd soap opera actually controls the destiny and experience of the total world of human beings—and that world-mummery is, in its root-disposition, totally indifferent to human life, and to the world altogether.

This fault in the human world has what could be called "philosophical" roots. There is a habit of mind and disposition that has taken over humankind. That habit of mind is ego-based. Therefore, egoity has taken over humankind—and egoity is being affirmed as "necessity" and "truth". This dreadful trend in human history is associated with a fixed philosophical "habit" that has been developing for centuries: the "habit" of "objectifying" the self and (altogether) "objectifying" both conditional reality and Reality Itself, and (then) identifying with that "objective" position—not only in mind, but in action. From that always "objectifying" position, everything (including Reality Itself) is viewed as an "object"—even the human self is viewed as an "object". That "objective" self is the reflected self, the self-idea that ego makes. It is "Narcissus". "Narcissus" is not self-aware—"Narcissus" is aware of self only as a reflection, and (thus and thereby) as if "other".

"Narcissus" is the nature of human society now. As a result, human society is becoming progressively more and more aggravated, and fundamentally dissociated from Reality Itself—leading to an absurd and insane life of competitive conflict for the totality of humankind. And that life of competitive conflict has already negatively affected even the natural systems of the Earth—and it is causing (and would continue to cause) terrible suffering everywhere.

The "objectifying" impulse also, of course, characterizes the view of "scientific materialism". "Science" (or the "scientific method") <u>itself</u> is simply <u>free</u> <u>enquiry</u>, without philosophical prejudices, and without fixed presumptions relative to "results" and "interpretations". However, rather than pure science, it is scientific materialism (or the philosophy of "objective materialism", enacted by means of a philosophically prejudiced control over the interpretations, and even the apparent results, of the application of the protocols of the scientific method) that now, in general, dominates the societies of humankind. Indeed, scientific materialism can rightly be said to be the root-philosophical basis for the justification of egoic society and ego-based living—because the orientation (and basic method) of scientific materialism is to first "objectify" any and every "subject", and, thus, to look at it as an "object". In other words, the method of scientific materialism is to "objectify", and dissociate from, the any "subject", and, then, to analyze it, dissect it, deconstruct it, and manipulate it in a totally "objective" manner—until, at last, Reality Itself becomes philosophically proposed (or psychologically supposed and presumed) to <u>be</u> merely "objective".

In the programmatic method of materialistic "objectification", the self, being part of Reality, is also viewed as "objective" (and reduced to the status of "object"). That effort is the program of "Narcissus". "Narcissus" even thinks of <u>himself</u>, or <u>herself</u>, as an "object". "Narcissus" only sees his or her own reflection, his or her mirrored persona—without recognizing it as such, and always thinking it is somebody "else".

Systematic "objectification" of self, and of even <u>all</u> of Reality, <u>is</u> the characteristic method of <u>egoity</u>. Thus, to <u>every</u>

ego-"I", self is "object". To itself, the ego-self is an "objective" thing—as if an "other", separate and "objective", even to itself. That is a tragic and self-destructive situation—both to the ego-based individual and to the totality of ego-based society. Ego-"I" is the self-deluded situation—both personal and collective. To "objectify" the self—and, thus and thereby, to "understand" self only from outside the subjective position itself, and as if self is someone "else", or as if self is "other" to one's own "point of view"—is madness. However, it is also a commonplace madness—because "Narcissus", the "objectified" self (always viewed and presumed as if from outside), is every ego-"I" (or every presumed-to-be separate and separative self).

To "objectify" the world is to dissociate from it. Indeed, truly, even what is apparently "outside" the self can, paradoxically, only be rightly understood from "inside" (or by means of an ego-transcending discipline, exercised within one's own inherently subjective position). However, in this "late-time" (or "dark" epoch), all of human culture and all of human society is based on the process of "objectification". Consequently, the Root-Condition (or the Perfectly Subjective Self-Condition) of Reality Itself is now lost in human-time— abandoned therein by mere and terminal "objectification".

The self is, by definition, not "objective". The self is, necessarily, entirely subjective. Therefore, all phenomena, all of experiential existence, must, necessarily, be understood at the root-subjective level (and, thus, perceived and understood from the inside to out). Experience cannot rightly be perceived and understood otherwise (or from the outside toward in). Once the world is "objectified", once the self is "objectified", once everything and everyone is "objectified", a state of dissociation and separation is absolutely (and always negatively) enforced. The world of ego and egoic society is based on this habit of dissociation—the habit of "objectification" of everything and everyone, including the self.

The restoration of sanity and Truth—or the restoration to Reality Itself—requires the overcoming of the self-deluded process or activity or event of self-"objectification". In the self-"objectified" ego-state, the self becomes a mere reflection, as if viewed from without.

In the egoic world, self-consciousness is not, in Truth, aware of <u>self</u> (as it <u>is</u>). Rather, in the egoic world, self-consciousness is aware as <u>self-image</u>—a mirrored image of self, constructed as if it were an "object" seen from <u>outside</u>. No "object"-consciousness is Real and right self-consciousness. Truly Real and right "self-consciousness" requires a capital "S" and a capital "C". Truly Real and right "Self-Consciousness" is Root-Consciousness—Consciousness <u>As</u> <u>Is</u>, or Consciousness <u>As</u> Itself. Consciousness <u>Itself</u> <u>Is</u> the Tacit Free (and Inherently egoless) Witness of all and everything that is apparently arising. Consciousness Itself is not (and cannot be) "objectified". Consciousness Itself is not (and cannot be) in the form of an "object"—or in the form of the conditional knowing (or the conditional knowledge) of "objects". Consciousness Itself— Which <u>Is</u> Reality Itself—is Prior to all-and-All. Therefore, the True Self-Position is Prior to all arising and all conditionality.

This understanding is the necessary basis for the <u>Realization</u> of Reality Itself. Reality Itself is the <u>only</u> basis for true sanity and well-being. The Prior Unity of the entire conditionally arising world, and the prior unity of humankind, originates (Non-"differently") from (and, therefore, <u>As</u>) the Prior (and Self-Evidently Divine) Self-Condition and Source-Condition— Which is <u>always</u> (and Always Already) Prior to "objectification", dissociation, separateness, and separativeness.

Therefore, the disposition that is true to Reality Itself is also the disposition that, in the context of ordinary human life, functions on the basis of prior unity—not on the basis of presumed non-unity (or dis-unity). The root of that transformation—from non-unity to prior unity—is the self-knowledge (or self-understanding) that transcends the "objectification" of self (manufactured by the egoic act of dissociation, wherein the self is merely reflected, as if seen from outside).

True self-knowledge is seeing self and world from inside. The "objectified" self is strange, mad, dissociated, detached, in trouble, threatened by mortality, threatened by a self-consciousness that is inherently revolting (even to the conscious awareness of the "objectified" self). Seen from outside, the "objectified" self-body—as if seen by another perceiving oneself—is revolting. In that case, the self is reduced to mere vulgarity, mere functionality. Its "selfness"-from-within—Prior to arising conditions, Prior to the seeing of self from outside—is lost. To see self from outside is to be negatively self-conscious—dissociated and detached. That "objectified" view of self comes to be associated with a vulgar sense of self—which is the gross, and merely physical, sense of self that arises from viewing self as if from outside.

When seen merely from outside, when reduced to the "outside view", the bodily self (or the self as the body-only) is rather vulgar and disgusting. As has been said, in vulgar reference to the mere functionality of the human body (when seen from outside), it is nothing but a "shit-machine". From the "point of view" of outside (or the position after and subordinate to the "asshole"), the body is disgusting and shameful. From the outside position, you are (always, first of all) looking at the "end-product" of a "shit-machine". From the "point of view" of inside (or the position prior and senior to the "asshole"), the process of bodily elimination is simply a naturally (or subjectively) pleasurable process of purification. The body is built (and, thus, also brain-"wired") to constantly purify itself—and, thereby, to enjoy the plea-surable sensation of relief and self-purity that is naturally associated with the entire cycle of right food-taking and the efficient bodily elimination of waste. When the body is rightly disciplined (by right diet, right sex-practice, and so on), such that it is properly self-conservative and efficiently eliminative, the body regularly enjoys a sense of natural well-being. There is nothing shameful about that. What is shameful (or ashamed) is the self-identification with the "end-product"—and, also, the collective human inability to properly and efficiently recycle the inevitable waste products associated with all human life-activity.

As soon as the body is "objectified" (or seen only as if from outside), then, instead of right participation in the eliminative process (or the perspective of the "shitting"), there is simply the "shit" (or the evidence of what the body discards from itself). That "outside view" is a grossly "objectified" view of self—a view that is inherently vulgar (or disgusting), and "dark", and detached.

That "dark", outside "object"-vision of self is the fixed "point of view" of "Narcissus". "Narcissus" is trapped within (and by) the fixed "point of view"—and, as a consequence of the fixed "point of view" (relative to time and space), attention is confined to outside, and to mere reflections, and to a vulgar, guilty, and chronically ashamed sense of existence. To go beyond that, the human being must be restored to his or her own intrinsic inwardness—and, thus and thereby, to "Locate" What Is the Real Nature (or Inherently egoless Self-Condition) of that intrinsic inwardness.

What is the Real nature of the subjective position? When the subjective position is rightly discovered and understood (at its Transcendental Root), everything that is apparently "objective" is seen As Is—rather than as seen from without, from the dissociated position.

The entire human world is, by tendency, ego-bound. And ego itself has now become idealized, as a result of a process of hundreds, and even thousands, of years of the "culturation" of human existence in the direction of "Narcissism" (or egoity)—to the point where, now, Consciousness Itself (and Reality—Itself and altogether) has become utterly "objectified" (as a "thing", materially caused, and of a merely conditional, separate, and time-bound nature). As a result, the human world is, now, entangled in a process of self-destruction that is on the verge of destroying life itself. That unspeakably dreadful result is the end-phenomenon of a false philosophy. Indeed, this is the "dark" time of that false philosophy. This is the "dark" time—the "end-time" of scientific materialism. Therefore, in order to move the human world from the "dark" destiny of "end-time" to a truly En-Light-ened destiny, there must be a relinquishment of false "objectified" views, as a necessary part of the political, social, and cultural transformation of the totality of humankind.

Scientific materialism is on the "wrong side" of the "asshole" of human experiential awareness. "Objectification"-culture is on the "wrong side"—or the merely reflected side, or the opposite, and opposing, and detached, or abstracted, or fundamentally non-participatory side—of everything. Scientific materialism and the totality of "objectification"-culture are on the "wrong side" because they assume the fixed position (and the fixed, separate, and, therefore, egoic "point of view") of the outside (rather than the participatory, non-separate, and Inherently egoless Self-Condition of the inside) of Reality Itself (and, thus, of Truth Itself).

Therefore, the cultural enforcement of the "objectification" of self and the "objectification" of life altogether must be thwarted—for the sake of one and all in (and As) Reality and in Truth. The process of "objectification" (and fixed "outsideness") must be undone—by Truth. That undoing by Truth is, essentially, what true moral and Spiritual transformation is about. The genuine regaining of the Transcendental and Spiritual and Inherently egoless Self-Position (Which Is Truth Itself and Reality Itself) requires (and more and more becomes) a moral and Spiritual transformation—"moral" meaning a transformation of livingness, that re-establishes human life in the universal context of Prior Unity (and in the global human context of the constant exercise of the working-presumption of prior unity). Therefore, the truly "moral" disposition is the cooperative disposition, the disposition of tolerance, the disposition of compassion, and the disposition-beyond-compassion, which is true peace.

3.

Conflict and destruction take all kinds of forms in the human world and in human history. There has already been a long chain of terrible tyrants in the human sphere—but people everywhere seem to be unaware of the fact that the latest tyrant is <u>everybody</u>—or "Everyman". The latest—and the <u>last</u>—tyrant is "Everyman". The last tyrant is "the people". In this "late-time", "the people" have, as a collective, become merely another ego-driven, manipulatable, chaotic, and entirely mad entity—a kind of lunatic "herd", a chaos of gross collectivity. That tyrannical "herd" is subject to the same whims and absurdities as any individual tyrant ever was or is. That terrible "herd" knows no limits—and even all and everything it merely thinks it "knows" is <u>not</u> Reality and Truth. The "herd" that "the people" have become is simply another tyrant—and the last to rise and fall in human-time.

The "tyranny of everybody" is what is happening <u>now</u>. In the now, every individual wallows in the "Narcissistic" self-idea, demanding immediate satisfaction of the every wanting-need and random impulse in the body-mind, and threatening all-and-All with "consequence"-to-come, if separate self is found still wanting or unsatisfied at end of any day. The "neighborhood wars" between all egos, tribes, and cults of "thing" are what is happening now. The private wars of "Everyman", the society of "Everyman", the religiosity of "Everyman", the "late-time" of "Everyman" is what is happening <u>now</u>. The "Everyman" is "Narcissus", the last tyrant—the ego itself. When the tyrant becomes <u>everybody</u>, that <u>is</u> the end-time. When the tyrant is just somebody-in-particular, then there are revolutions, ups and downs and cycles. However, at the last, when the tyrant becomes everybody, there are no more cycles, but only a linearity of sames—and everyone and everything disintegrates in stops. Such is the awful nature of the present time, of ego's rule of all.

Therefore, it is <u>absolutely</u> <u>urgent</u> that there be an <u>immediate</u> and <u>total</u> transformation at the root of human culture and society and politics. A new kind of human institution must emerge in the world—an institution that truly establishes a <u>Global</u> <u>Cooperative</u> <u>Order</u>. That new (and, necessarily, global) institution must establish and enact a non-tyrannical (and even counter-tyrannical, or entirely post-tyrannical) order of rightly and effectively functioning cooperation between <u>everyone</u>—between <u>all</u> nations, between <u>all</u> cultures and tribes, between <u>all</u> the "neighborhoods".

What is required is not a matter of merely "having a dialogue" and "working toward" unity. In any such effort of "working toward", there is, in all the works, still plenty of effort to <u>dominate</u>. Therefore, what is required is the <u>establishment</u> of the <u>universal</u> working-presumption of prior unity—such that "the people", in every guise, lay down their arms, lay down their conflicts and their aggressive competitiveness, and, on that basis, <u>straightforwardly</u> handle all the business that is in the interest of <u>everybody</u> <u>altogether</u>.

That "handling of business" is not being done at the present time. Now, everybody is "on the brink" with everybody else. It is everywhere like that. The "daily news" is that. Everyone's daily life has become something like an insane sporting event—that is played to the death. The human world of nowtime is like colossal Reality-TV—a dreadful mini-series, a few weeks until death. The common world of nowtime is mere insanity—Reality-madness. Everyone and everything is mad with "Everyman" now—mad with ego, mad with "Narcissus". The <u>last</u> tyrant is <u>everybody</u>—everybody at war with everybody, to the death.

If this mad world-mummery continues unchecked, the present time of human history <u>is</u> the <u>end</u> of humantime. It is no longer a matter of one principal tyrant somewhere, some head of state somewhere, who is the "whomever", or the "whatever", that everyone loves to hate as everybody's "enemy". In this "late-time" (or "dark" epoch), <u>everybody</u> is the "enemy". <u>Everybody</u> is wrong. <u>Everybody</u> is at fault. <u>Everybody</u> is "Narcissus". <u>Everybody</u> is "Everyman". "Everyman" is everywhere. The "objectified" self is at large. If "Everyman" is not soon disciplined by the Truth That Is Reality Itself—so that the world of "Everyman" discovers and accepts "its" limits, "its" place—then "Everyman" is going to destroy not only humankind but all life, and the Earth-world itself.

4.

The always globalizing (or would-be-all-inclusive) culture and civilization of genuinely human humankind is being lost and forgotten in the "herd" and rush of present-time at fault. In very fundamental terms, it must be said that genuinely human culture has <u>already</u> been lost, through a terrible "progress", especially over the last few hundred years—and that, only "lately", has gone truly "dark" (within a mere and fatal one hundred years). Just look at the century of recent past: The twentieth century was the deadliest, most murderous century in the history of humankind—and, yet, coincidentally, it is also the century of the greatest "advancements" in the scientific materialist domain of "objectification"-culture.

There are, obviously, many results of <u>truly</u> scientific endeavor that are positive, in the sense of fostering, and supporting, and extending from human well-being. Nevertheless, the "objectification"-effort of <u>materialistic</u> scientism is a <u>fundamental</u>, and generally negative (and power-hungry), characteristic of the "Everyman"-culture of this "late-time".

The reductionistic materialism of this all-"objectifying" epoch of "late-time" is fundamentally negative in its philosophical roots, and, therefore, never truly and wholly positive in either its "point of view" or its interpretations or its results. The "late-time" effort of materialistic (and all-"objectifying") scientism is the ego-effort of cleverness, magnified virtually infinitely—even beyond the limit of any right purpose of human usefulness. It is the "objectification" mind-culture, gaining control through merely "objective" (and altogether and reductively materialistic, and even inwardly thus reductive) knowledge—exercising control over self and "other" and world, and exercising control over virtually everything in the ordinary physical domain. That cleverness has produced a kind of mad "intelligence"—and a mad "book of its knowings". That "book" has a degree and kind of authenticity—but, at the same time, that "book" is an expression of the ego-bound mind that has "objectified" <u>itself</u>, to the point where it no longer knows <u>itself</u>, except by <u>reflection</u>. The merely reflected self is detached—and it knows no bounds, and it knows no Truth, other than what it merely <u>thinks</u> is "Truth" on the basis of having "objectified" <u>everything</u>.

There is nothing merely negative, in and of itself, about true scientific practice and knowledge. What is negative about science is its revisioning (or its reductive re-formulation) as "scientific <u>materialism</u>". Scientific materialism is the ultimate extension of "Narcissistic" culture. Therefore, the enterprise and culture of science must, like all other human enterprises, be brought into the sphere of Truth—and of Perfectly Subjective Reality Itself—or else mere science, like any other merely clever method of mind, simply becomes an instrument of illusion (or of self-delusion), and of potential destruction.

The restoration (to Itself) of the Perfectly Subjective State of Consciousness Itself is <u>essential</u>. There <u>must</u> be the globalized transcending of "point-of-view" culture, or "objectification"-culture—and the transcending, therefore, of all dissociation, all separateness, all non-unity. The reductionist justification for "objectification"-culture must be here and now undone, by a comprehensive root-understanding—or else the "last tyrant" will destroy the world.

In order that world-destruction be prevented, the "late-time" ego-culture must be stopped in its tracks. The pond-water into which Narcissus is gazing must be stirred to deep. The merely surface-made reflection must be broken up. And all the people of the humankind must be restored (in their understanding, and, ultimately, Most Perfectly) to the Perfectly Subjective Reality-State That <u>Is</u> Always Already the Case. In the context of that restoration, ordinary and also truly scientific (or truly <u>freely</u> enquiring) knowing of all kinds is appropriate, useful, and potentially beneficial—

including what could otherwise be said to be of the nature of truly discriminative "objective" knowledge. When the enterprises of conditional knowledge take place in the context of the Truth of Perfect Subjectivity (or of Reality Itself), then conditional knowledge has the virtue of inherent limits, and the discipline of right situation—and, on that basis, the exercise of conditional knowing is not functioning merely on a self-deluded basis, and, thus, dissociatively or destructively (such as is, necessarily, the case when no depth of Truth, or of Reality Itself, is Intrinsically Known).

The Depth of Truth (or of Reality Itself) must be established as the <u>basis</u> of life—not merely as the <u>goal</u> of life. That Depth is the necessary <u>basis</u> of right culture, and not merely the <u>goal</u> of ego-culture. That Depth must become the <u>everyday</u> Truth—such that It transforms everyday experience for everyone.

5.

I am not speaking of all of this in merely utopian terms—as if transforming the world were simply a matter of giving a lecture. A very practical means for contacting everybody, and getting everybody involved in what is new and right, must be precisely organized and consistently put to practical collective global use. (Perhaps the "Internet" can thus be made to serve? And why not a thus reformed—and no longer "Dis-United and Divided and Competitive and Confrontational"—"United Nations", too?) By thus actually globally organizing humankind in a dialogue with itself, all of humankind can make right and positive changes all over the world—and, thus, everywhere require a positive rightness, and everywhere require an end to conflict, and everywhere require an end of all seeking for global dominance (or otherwise negative dominance) by whomever and whatever would seek it.

At this critical turning-point in human history, certain "lessons" must be accepted from the errors and the tragedies of past-time human faults. Among those "lessons", there is, certainly, one principal issue that must be accepted as a universal Law of humankind: No one—and no nation or culture on Earth—has a right, or any license in Reality Itself, to plan, or equip themselves to make, or at any time to materially enact any global or otherwise mass destruction, for any reason or purpose whatsoever, now or ever in humantime.

Therefore, rather than playing the global competition-game to its terrible end, like gangs of adolescents at deadly sport, there must be the establishment of a true Global Cooperative Forum, based on the working-presumption and enactment of prior unity—and, thus and thereby, the globally-extended establishment of a no-nonsense, getting-down-to-business disposition and practice in humankind at large. And, in this Global Cooperative Forum (and Right Order) of humankind, everyone will—and, indeed, must—focus on the genuine necessary issues that everyone has in common.

6.

A Global Cooperative Forum <u>must</u> be established—a forum that includes <u>everybody</u>, and <u>all</u> nations, without national boundaries, and (altogether) without political, social, or institutional barriers of any kind. It would, thus, be the Global Cooperative Forum (and thereby established and perpetuated Right Order) of <u>all</u> of humankind.

The purpose and responsibility of the Global Cooperative Forum would be to establish a working-agenda, and (on that basis) to systematically and efficiently deal with every kind of issue that is fundamental to right life and supportive of all life, and (thus) to address the rightening of all the terrible things that are "in the works" everywhere—including the pandemic of negative global competitiveness, dissociative warrior-nationalisms, the "sport" of strategic war-making, the everywhere aggressive search for global dominance by corporations and traditional institutions, and all the overwhelming changes now progressing in the natural domain, including global warming and climate change, the global epidemics of disease and poverty, the global depletion of natural resources, the global pervasiveness of toxic wastes, the global dependence on archaic practical and political and social and human-resource technologies and methods, and so on, and on.

The humankind-culture of this "late-time" is the global drama of dis-united nations—or the competitive nations of the world. Such is a kind of absurd global gladiatorial contest. On the other hand, when the universal working-presumption is <u>prior</u> unity (or <u>inherent</u> indivisibility), then humankind will not come together merely to try to dominate one another or play off of one another. <u>Nobody</u> has, or can have, that kind of dominance when there is a Global Cooperative Forum based on the working-presumption of prior unity. Therefore, when everybody comes to a seat in the Global Cooperative Forum that is about the working-presumption of prior unity, all the dramatization of self-prominence of the "objectified" personality, whether personal or national, is specifically and totally undermined. The habits and games of ego-posturing have no place to sit or shout in the Global Cooperative Forum.

When prior unity is presumed, everybody has a different face than that of "Narcissus". When prior dis-unity is presumed, everybody has a mummer's ego-face—everybody is playing a faker's role, everybody is wearing a deceitful costume, everybody is getting their "15 minutes of fame" on TV, by playing on the latest possibility of "daily news".

All of that "TV of Narcissus" is utterly obnoxious and passé—and the signs in the world all prove it is far too late in the human course for humankind to be going on with that nonsense anymore. All of that simply must stop.

The national and institutional and otherwise corporate leaderships all over the world are, at the present time, merely playing on the "objectified"-self-culture of "Everyman", and playing off one another like adolescent goons—as if the world is all a meaningless game of gross consumption and excessive waste, and as if it all is made especially for their own glamour to be seen, and made the "Narcissistic object" of all eyes. Therefore, those "in power" must be everywhere awakened to right responsibility—by everybody else. On the basis of that awakening, all the leaders in the world must become directly and consistently accountable to the now and future billions of humankind as a whole—and such that all who are given leadership responsibilities in the world always act as the true and globally accountable servants of all of humankind.

To play absurd games with the human and natural world is, now and forever hereafter, simply not acceptable. Time is up. Such nonsense must be given no more space and time.

7.

I f <u>everyone</u> worldwide is involved in the Global Cooperative Forum—not just localized, but <u>truly</u> globalized—then a single global demand will be made on <u>everybody</u> in power, <u>everywhere</u> <u>at</u> <u>once</u>.

There should simply be a rightly managed global cooperative process, in which every individual has particular responsibilities in the global totality. <u>Right</u> human life is not about <u>anybody</u> being exclusively and unaccountably "in power". The conducting of human affairs must, as a practical matter, necessarily be focused through individuals, institutions, and workable systems—but, when human politics is conformed to a right global mechanism for doings (founded on the constantly applied working-presumption of prior unity), then politics will have an altogether rightened face and characteristic. Any treachery would be undermined immediately, in the Global Cooperative Forum. Any treachery would lose its footing—<u>immediately</u>—in the Global Cooperative Forum.

Such right human politics would not result in any kind of absolute state of social perfection—or "utopia". Human beings <u>cannot</u> do <u>everything</u>. But they <u>can</u> do <u>much</u>—since so much of what everyone is suffering is, itself, the result of human activity. Whatever is humanly caused can be redressed in a very positive sense—such that the energies of humankind are put to solving the real problems, and <u>immediately</u> <u>stopping</u> the global absurdity of conflict and mummery.

Human society is not—and never will be—utopia. There is always the negative <u>and</u> the positive. However, the <u>exclusively</u> negative is now globalized. It is overwhelming. It is everywhere. It is everyone. Therefore, the situation <u>itself</u> must be <u>replaced</u>, by a new situation, based on global cooperation.

<u>Who</u> must make and do the Global Cooperative Forum (and the Global Cooperative Order) of humankind?

Everyone. You—the people of the world. Every one of "Every-man" must be changed, and restored to the non-dissociative circumstance—not just to a change of thought, but to a change in doings, a change of participation, engaged in a truly global place. Everyone must get together—without the unfruitful overlay of the dissociative consciousness of merely "objectified" personality—and get on with what is necessary for the well-being and survival of everyone and everything.

No nonsense—just get on with it.

That is, fundamentally, what there is to say about it.

PART EIGHT

Wash All The Flags
(and Leave All Name-Tags
and Placards At the Door)

1.

In international affairs, virtually everyone speaks from a "point of view" that is associated with the interests of a particular national State. Everyone is propagandizing something on the basis of a national identity—or, more generally, on the basis of an identity related to some religious, cultural, social, or political institution. In any such case, the basis for political discourse is the prior presumption of a limited identity (or "objectified" self-image) that is less than the totality of humankind. This is the fundamental cause of many of the world's problems.

The principle of right and true civilization requires that everyone must always assume the disposition of being part of humankind <u>first</u>. <u>That</u> is the necessary and indispensable basis for right human (or civilized) discourse. The disposition of being part of humankind <u>first</u> means taking the "point of view" of totality and universality. It does not require dissociation from one's nation, one's birthplace, or one's particular citizenship. Rather, it requires the discipline of always exercising a disposition that, fundamentally, transcends any kind of particularity of orientation, and which looks at all human problems as part of humankind's inherently global concerns, without any other "angle" on it whatsoever. In that disposition—and only on the basis of that truly civilized self-discipline—the world's problems can be dealt with straightforwardly and effectively, in concrete and practical terms.

The disposition of always (and inherently) being part of humankind <u>first</u> implies a kind of egolessness. Of course, that disposition is still associated with a conditional (human) identity. Therefore, that disposition is still a kind of egoity. That disposition is not equivalent to any form of Spiritual or Transcendental Enlightenment. Nevertheless, the working-disposition of being part of the totality of humankind inherently (and actively) transcends (or exceeds) the separate and separative "point of view" of the usual participation in the world-business of human happenings.

There are many levels of conditional identity that are commonly presumed: the personal identity, the localized (or immediate) identity (of life-associations, upbringing, family, and village), and the national and religious and racial identities. All these images of "self", or "points of view", encumber everyone's understanding—but they are, characteristically, the first thing that everyone puts out in front. Everyone is, by tendency, always mumming a collection of self-images—or the conventionally "objectified" persona with which each one, ordinarily, tends to identify. Whenever anyone says "I", that "objectified" ego-persona is who they mean.

Nevertheless, if everyone is (as a working-presumption of moral self-discipline) always part of humankind first, then that universal context becomes the basis for examining everything. Taking that universal "point of view" inherently and inevitably cools all the potential violence of the discourse of self-imagery. On that basis, cooperation and tolerance are made possible, because everyone agrees not to assume their separative identities first—or, at least, everyone agrees to actively assume the rather universal identity of being part of the totality of humankind. In that case, each human being can participate with all other human beings in simply handling the business everyone has in common. Starting from that universal "point of view", the discussion can focus, in a straightforward manner, on all the issues associated with particularities—including national matters. But all such issues must be addressed in the context of the totality of humankind, rather than in the context of all the lesser (separate and separative) identities, and all the strategizing (verbal, and otherwise) that comes with those identities.

This, therefore, is the necessary implication of being part of a Global Cooperative Forum of humankind as a whole:

the obligation and responsibility to go beyond the separate and separative identity (or self-image) associated with the "point of view" of conventional living—whether personal and local, or in the somewhat enlarged sphere of one's "tribal" situation or national State. The establishment of this basis for universal discourse is absolutely essential. That is what the Global Cooperative Forum allows and enables, and why it has a (potentially, global) corrective or balancing effect. However, what is currently reflected in ordinary daily life, as well as in the discourse of the "daily news", is "point-of-view" language, based on all the different modes of self-imagery. Everybody is speaking via a self-image that is less than the totality of humankind—and every such self-image is in opposition to even every other self-image. Thus, the usual discourse is confrontation-language.

Conventional discourse is a kind of theatre, or role-playing. It is mummery. The Global Cooperative Forum makes it possible to transcend this mummery—this merely "dramatic" discourse between assumed identities (or self-images). The Global Cooperative Forum inherently transcends all such mummery, by providing a uniquely free mode of discourse. In the Global Cooperative Forum, the rules of discourse will be very different from the rules of discourse in a forum where identity (or self-image) is presumed to be the basis for exchanges. As long as limited identity (rather than universal identity) is the basis for discourse, the language is all "plus" and "minus": confrontation-language, or language based on presumed differences. In that case, very little resolution is possible—because everyone is trying to "win", or to "save face".

In the Global Cooperative Forum, there is no "face" to be "saved". Therefore, fundamental to the virtue of the Global Cooperative Forum is that it is not based on limited self-imagery. It transcends mummery. It transcends the identity of common egoity—by simply setting that identity aside.

2.

Discourse in the Global Cooperative Forum would have different rules than the rules of conventional discourse. There are "rules of order" in any mode of "institutionalized" discourse, and the Global Cooperative Forum is a kind of institutional setting for human discourse. Therefore, the Global Cooperative Forum must have order and rules. It must be organized so as to be practically effective—and all of the details must be spelled out: How is the Global Cooperative Forum to be made practical? How are representation and participation to be organized? What are the rules of discourse, and the "rules of order"?

The fundamental principle governing discourse in the Global Cooperative Forum is the setting aside of the projection of limited identity—whether that identity is based on factors local to one's life-situation or on one's national, racial, or religious associations. In the circumstance of participation in the Global Cooperative Forum, no mode of limited association is to be made into a "label". In the Global Cooperative Forum, such modes of association have no intrinsic significance. Certain local issues (national, racial, religious, or otherwise) may need to be addressed in the Global Cooperative Forum—but discourse within the Global Cooperative Forum should not be based on the "identity-labels" associated with such local issues.

The Global Cooperative Forum is different from any international institution that has existed up to now. No one would "sit at" the Global Cooperative Forum. In the Global Cooperative Forum, people would not have placards in front of them, announcing their national identity as the basis for discourse. The fundamental "label" each one would have is "human being"—and nothing else. Thus, the Global Cooperative Forum has an entirely different basis for its discourse. It is not "hot" discourse—it is "cool" discourse.

By eliminating all the usual "labels", the self-imagery that creates differences is eliminated out front—such that a cool, or (in the right sense) objective, "point of view" can be established that can deal with real issues in a straightforward manner—without ego-identity becoming the basis. In that case, the discourse focuses on the subject matter to be addressed—not "hotly debated", but rather coolly considered, because no limited identity is presumed as the basis. Thus, the Global Cooperative Forum is the active world-consideration based on the prior unity of everyone—priorly established, and (therefore) not debated.

The purpose of the Global Cooperative Forum is not to create more status and further differences. Nothing of that kind should be established. There are no separate "flags" in the Global Cooperative Forum. The Global Cooperative Forum is not there in the form of confrontation with anyone. It relinquishes confrontation in principle. No confrontation, no war, no self-imagery beyond that of being part of the totality of humankind, and having the entire globe as the domain in which to consider all issues.

3.

There is no stark difference between the human species and all other species. There is a prior unity present in the world as a whole. There is obviously a specific orientation that characterizes human beings as human beings in civilized discourse. But, as a human being, recognizing the prior unity of the world, you must have concern for Earth itself, and all the species within it, all life within it, all structures and forms and processes that are part of the world, including all the non-humans.

This does not mean one should view non-humans as if they were humans. Rather, this means one should view humans as part of a larger whole. That is the necessary basis for considering issues that have to do with non-humans as well as humans—as well as issues related to the environment, and to all other aspects of the world. Humankind has the entire Earth as its province—and, therefore, humankind must deal with issues that have to do with what is of the Earth, and with what is associated with non-human species. Humankind must function rightly and compassionately for all.

Human beings have the ability to conceive and voice issues that relate to the Earth and to the non-human species. On that basis, human beings must address issues that relate to the Earth and non-human species, and human beings must do so rationally and compassionately.

Therefore, such matters are also part of all the issues that would be considered by the Global Cooperative Forum. Everything of Earth—everything non-human as well as everything human. And even everything beyond the Earth that human beings can affect—for example, through space exploration. These matters need to be engaged on the basis of right principles, and not merely become the basis for more conflicts. Conflict and confrontation are endless when non-unity and self-imagery prevail. You can make the universe a mummery just as you can make Earth a mummery. The ego makes mummery—and egolessness transcends mummery. Therefore, the Global Cooperative Forum, by its very nature, must operate on the non-egoic principle, on the principle of the prior transcending of self-imagery.

The Global Cooperative Forum—by definition, and by necessity—is all-inclusive and non-confrontational.

4.

The Global Cooperative Forum would not eliminate existing national, social, religious, or political institutions. That is not the point. But the Global Cooperative Forum is about cooperation between all these institutions—and the basis for that cooperation is a kind of "tabula rasa" (or clean slate), without self-imagery, as the circumstance in which to engage (with all others) in an address to common human problems.

The common (or global and universal) human problems are what the Global Cooperative Forum needs to actively address—because, while everybody is fussing with the latest mummer's drama of the "daily news", things are deteriorating more and more profoundly in areas that (because of the constant diversions made of human nonsense) are not being addressed directly and effectively: the overall condition of the Earth, environmental pollution, global warming, climate change, the abuse of power by corporations and governments, the necessity for new technologies and new methods in every area of human life, the scarcity of fuel resources and of natural and human resources altogether, disease, famine, poverty, overpopulation, urbanization, globalization, human migration, territorial disputes, violent crime, the pervasive accumulation (and the sometimes actual use) of excessively (and even catastrophically) destructive weapons, the tendency of national States to avoid cooperation and mutual accommodation, the tendency of national States (or factions within national States) to use war (and, otherwise, unspeakably dark-minded violence) as a method for achieving the goals of national and otherwise culturally idealized policies, and so on—and on. Human inventiveness must be released from the perpetual self-imposition of mummery (or false, and, otherwise, unnecessary, human drama), that undermines the ability of humankind to handle its right and necessary (and, now, urgent) business.

The "daily news" is about the inventing of drama and oppositions. That is what the news media always tend to do. The news media tend always to look for the "differences", the "opposites", the basis for controversy and confrontation, in order to make a human drama (and even a form of popular entertainment) out of it. Drama is the working-principle of the "daily news". However, that is <u>not</u> the principle of the Global Cooperative Forum. "No-drama" is the principle of the Global Cooperative Forum—no opposition, no differences, no controversy, no nonsense, and only "business handled".

5.

There is no place for "warrior-kings" and "high-mucky-mucks" in the Global Cooperative Forum. There necessarily must be representatives, but the representatives must be disciplined by the people (and the necessary civilization-principles) they represent. In other words, these representatives have to be able to set aside their self-imagery, their conventional identity—their "name-tags", and "flags", and "placards", and "slogans"—and deal with real practical issues, as true servants of the total all of humankind. There can be any number of such servant-representatives, but, as such, none of them are "warrior-kings" or "high-mucky-mucks". In the Global Cooperative Forum, there is no room for the "one-group-over-against-another-group" mentality. By definition, and by necessity, the Global Cooperative Forum operates on the basis of the absolute, prior, and tacit equality of all. The necessary governing-agreement is that there are no "warrior-kings", no "high-mucky-mucks", and no senior (or, otherwise, subordinate) factions.

If differences are presumed from the beginning, effective discourse can only proceed a short distance. However, if one begins by making no differences at all, effective discourse can proceed to an unlimited degree. Such is the basis for the Global Cooperative Forum: There are no differences, no "seniors" over against "juniors", no subordinates with others above them. There is an "equal table", in which everyone participates, and where representation is simply a means for making the Global Cooperative Forum able, as a practical matter, to function effectively (and in the interests of everyone equally).

Literally everyone should participate in the Global Cooperative Forum. However, to make it orderly, so that it can function effectively, some individuals must, by necessity, have key representational functions within it. If any of those individuals start "putting on" their self-imagery too prominently, they would have to be addressed and disciplined. They would have to be disciplined by the whole, and be able to accept that, and always "wash their flags".

The ability to "lose face" is fundamental to being able to function rightly in the context of the Global Cooperative Forum. You cannot show up as an ego, full of self-imagery of any kind—personal, racial, religious, national, or whatever it may be. You cannot manifest that, and be anything like a principal individual serving as a significant representative of everyone via the Global Cooperative Forum. Therefore, all who function as representatives in the Global Cooperative Forum must constantly "wash their flags". Individuals serving within the Global Cooperative Forum must constantly drop whatever they may inadvertently (or, otherwise, strategically) introduce that would establish a principle of difference, or that represents a self-image that would cause the exclusion of some element of humankind's concerns, or the exclusion of any dimension of human existence.

To participate productively in the Global Cooperative Forum does not mean an individual cannot have personal views that are otherwise particularized—such as, for example, a personal association with a particular religious tradition. However, participation in the Global Cooperative Forum does mean (and require) that an individual must not allow any particular self-image (or mode of personal association) to be the active basis for his or her participation in the Global Cooperative Forum itself. All self-imagery must be set aside, so that the individual does not even function secretly or unconsciously on a separate and separative and counter-productive basis. Everyone who participates in the Global Cooperative Forum must be able to simply assume the prior identity of "human being"—without "flags", without self-imagery otherwise—and to look at everything and everyone, at all issues and all problems that need to be addressed, in a straightforward and unprejudiced manner.

The Global Cooperative Forum is—by definition, and by necessity—constantly self-correcting. Therefore, individuals who can function most flexibly in such a circumstance would be the best people to occupy the principal representative positions that are needed to enable the Global Cooperative Forum to be effective.

Obviously, the confrontational orientation to discourse cannot work in the setting of the Global Cooperative Forum itself. To carry on the process (or global human business) of the Global Cooperative Forum, the participating representatives must be able to relinquish the confrontational disposition, and, yet, still know what are the real human concerns that need to be addressed. Individuals who have a confrontational "talent" would either have to be able to set it aside to participate in this Global Cooperative Forum, or they would have to function in a different role relative to it perhaps by providing relevant information relative to certain issues. But those who function in the role of participatory representation (of humankind as a whole) within the Global Cooperative Forum, and who, therefore, as a practical matter, must carry on its process, must be (in real practice) free of the confrontational disposition. In that sense, they must be talented "diplomats". They must know how to carry on really effective discourse while (as a really effective self-discipline) relinquishing the confrontational attitude, and they must, on that basis, be all-inclusive in their active disposition. It is not merely about having a "poker face"—or a false face, that merely hides a limited and all-limiting self-image. Rather, it is about being able to maintain the discipline of non-confrontation—and to really (and always rightly) make things happen, always now.

PART NINE

723

The Free Declaration of
The Universal Moral, Social,
and Political Laws of
True and Necessary Civilization

f, as it is commonly supposed, national States have an inherent right to defend (and even to expand) themselves, the people (and the human species itself) have the same inherent right—and the self-responsible duty to exercise it. If this were not so, where would national States have acquired the right otherwise?

A living species (or even any living entity or individual) is, itself, <u>naturally</u> motivated merely toward survival (by means of reproduction, struggle, domination, and expansion). Only a <u>civilization-culture</u> makes <u>morality</u> and <u>Wisdom</u>. Among all the living species now on Earth, only the human species makes (or, indeed, can make) civilization-cultures. All right human morality is based on the (uniquely) human (and, therefore, mind-based and memory-dependent) capability for the comprehension of <u>totality</u> and <u>universality</u>.

<u>All</u> war is now genocide. The people—and not merely the national armies of national States—are now the targets of <u>all</u> wars. Therefore, the people—<u>everywhere</u> and <u>all</u> <u>together</u>—must have (and must exercise) the right to approve or disapprove (and, thus and thereby, to allow or not allow) the activities (of war, and of everything else) proposed and exercised by each and every national government of State.

Right laws—based not merely on naturally self-based and grossly survival-oriented motives, but, rather, on the truly <u>moral</u> exercise of universal and all-including, and, thus, really civilized, principles—must <u>everywhere</u> govern <u>both</u> the people <u>and</u> the national States. Therefore, a <u>Global Cooperative Order</u> of <u>all</u> of humankind, "voiced" through the exercise of truly universal and all-including principles, must, now, and forever hereafter, be the root-context of <u>all</u> national States.

People take refuge (and citizenship) in a national State because they (by <u>inherent</u> <u>right</u>) expect the national State to <u>guarantee</u> and <u>actively</u> <u>uphold</u> their necessary basic human rights to <u>unlimited physical participation</u> (in all basic political, social, cultural, and economic processes) and to <u>unlimited</u> <u>protection</u> <u>from</u> <u>physical</u> <u>violence</u> (whether violence is directed from <u>within</u> the national State, in the form of crime, or from outside the national State, in the form of war). Therefore, <u>every</u> national State (or sovereign political entity) <u>must</u> (by necessity, by law, and by universal agreement) guarantee and uphold these necessary expectations (and inherent rights) of each and all of their citizens, residents, and visitors.

Unlimited physical participation and unlimited physical protection are the necessary basic human rights of all human beings within the boundaries of any civilized national State. These rights are not merely "natural" in their nature or origin. Rather, these rights are, in their nature and origin, expressions of the comprehension of totality and universality. Therefore, these rights are of the nature of civilization, and they must originate from civilization—and they can (and will) be guaranteed and actively upheld <u>only</u> by truly civilized national States.

The entire world of humankind must enter into a <u>perpetual</u> global dialogue (via a Global Cooperative Forum), and, thus and thereby, establish (and actively perpetuate) a Global Cooperative Order based on mutual cooperation, tolerance, real peace, and the principle of <u>prior</u> unity. In this manner, <u>all</u> national States must (in a global dialogue with the <u>thus</u> "righteous voice of the people") be brought to agree to function as <u>civilized</u> national States, and, thus and thereby, to <u>absolutely</u> guarantee and to <u>always</u> <u>actively</u> uphold the two necessary basic human rights (of unlimited physical participation and unlimited physical protection) within their national boundaries. Likewise, all <u>such</u> (<u>thus</u> civilized) national States must conform themselves to (and, thus, remain <u>always</u> <u>subordinate</u> <u>to</u>) the "righteous voice of the people"—expressed collectively via the always continuous Global Cooperative Forum of <u>all</u> of humankind.

Civilized national States have neither the inherent right nor the inherent calling to either guarantee or actively uphold any kind of presumed emotional or mental human "rights", but only necessary basic physical human rights. Thus, in the context of civilized society, the conditions associated with human emotional and/or mental processes and modes of expression must not be associated with pro-active manipulations, rules, and limits, but, rather, with pro-active freedoms and allowances—and a general environment of limitlessness.

The human right of unlimited physical participation must, necessarily, include unlimited physical access to all modes of education, culture, free exchange, responsibility-training, and Wisdom-learning—but, in order for all of that physical access to be right, effective, and truly unlimited, it must, itself, be truly free, really demanding, and of an all-inclusive nature. Therefore, no civilized national State should establish or enforce any limiting controls on the emotional and/or mental expressiveness of human beings and human institutions within their boundaries—except insofar as any emotional or mental demonstration in physical action threatens, causes, or enacts a limitation on the necessary and basic physical human rights of anyone (including the would-be limitation-doers themselves).

Thus, all civilized national States must refrain from the establishing and the enforcing of any laws or procedures that limit the free physical and verbal expression of emotional feelings and/or mental conceptions within their national boundaries. In that case, all civilized national States must establish and uphold laws and procedures that guarantee and enforce unlimited free speech, unlimited free emotional expression, and unlimited free physical activity—except insofar as any mode of speech or of emotional expression threatens physical harm on anyone (including the would-be harm-doers themselves), and, also, insofar as any mode of physical activity threatens, causes, or enacts physical harm on anyone (including the would-be harm-doers themselves), and, altogether, insofar as any mode of speech or of emotional expression or of physical activity threatens, causes, or enacts a limitation on the necessary basic human rights of anyone (including the would-be limitation-doers themselves). The Global Cooperative Forum of all of humankind must perpetually insist and always actively and lawfully require that every national State accept, and guarantee, and actively uphold all these requirements for civilized national Statehood, including the real, active, and consistent conformity and subordination (or self-responsible self-disciplining) of the every national State to the "righteous voice of the people" expressed collectively via the Global Cooperative Forum of all of humankind. Likewise, and coincidently, the "righteous voice of the people" must be really, actively, and consistently conformed and subordinated to the principles of the necessary basic human rights, and, altogether, the Global Cooperative Order of all of humankind must be conformed and subordinated to the principle of civilization— which principle requires real, active, and consistent conformity and subordination (or self-responsible self-disciplining) of every human individual to the inherently ego-transcending comprehension of totality and universality.

On this basis, the Global Cooperative Forum of all of humankind must constantly and uncompromisingly demand (and always actively and lawfully require) the real, total, and universal global national-State-enactment (or civilization-culture-fulfillment) of the principle of the physical protection of all of humankind—and, as a support for the necessary physical environment on which the physical protection of all of humankind must naturally depend, the physical protection of the Earth-world as a whole (and even the physical protection of the natural order of the universe within which the Earth-world is appearing and on which it depends) must, likewise, be demanded, required, and enacted.

This is the Free Declaration, for one and for all, of what is right and necessary for humankind in its now much advanced stage of global collective development, and of universal mutuality, and of universal mutual dependence—and of universal mutual aggravation and suffering.

The <u>old</u> moral, social, and political "order" of humankind <u>is</u> now dead. A new and true and right Way of order of humankind is, now, and forever hereafter, necessary. <u>This</u> Free Declaration is the Seed-Utterance of that new and necessary Way of true and right (and truly globally, totally, and universally cooperative) order.

<u>This</u> moment in human-time—July 23, 2006—is the precise and decisive moment of the uniquely new human necessity for <u>all</u> of humankind. Therefore, all signs say and illustrate that, if the new Way of true and right and truly human civilization herein and hereby Freely Declared is not now and everywhere chosen and enacted, the return to a natural and ego-based and inherently immoral chaos of separateness, division, mutual opposition, deadly competition, global conflagration, universal suffering, universal darkness, and universal death will have its global mandate of indifference—to move by nature's "twos" of human species' double-minded left and right of hands, to terminally and conclusively replace the civilization of this always fateful all of humankind.

One and all, consider <u>this</u> Free Declaration of your possibility on Earth.

One and all, <u>Be</u> of this Free Wisdom Blessed and made <u>all</u> right—together and at once.

PART TEN

I̲s-Peace

1.

R eality Itself will not "Save" you.
Reality Itself Is "Salvation".
Inherent Freedom Is the Liberation-Gift Reality
Itself here-Shows to all-and-All.

Before and Where an "object" or an ego-"I" becomes defined to any "point of view", A Perfect Mirror Always Stands—Awake.

That Perfect Mirror Is the One and Indivisible Real (and here-Acausal) God of all-and-All.

2.

"God"-ideas (and even all mere ideas) are ego-based "objectifications" (or Self-Reflected Self-Images) of the Intrinsic (and Inherently egoless) Self-Consciousness of Reality Itself—and, therefore, of Intrinsically Self-Evident (and Inherently egoless) Real Self (Itself).

No mere "God"-ideas Are Real (Acausal) God.

Only Reality Itself (and, therefore, Intrinsically Self-Evident and Inherently egoless Real Self, or Reality-Self, Itself) Is Real (Acausal) God.

Therefore, "God"-ideas (and even all mere ideas) must be (and, indeed, Always Already are) Transcended in, by Means of, and As Reality (Itself) and Real Self (Itself).

Real Self (or Reality-Self)—or the always first and always present Self-Condition of Conscious Awareness—Is Intrinsically Self-Evident As the Indivisible and Never-Broken Current of Feeling-Energy-Consciousness.

Within the Always Prior and Senior Context of the Intrinsically Self-Evident (and Self-Evidently egoless, and Spiritual, and Transcendental) Current of Real Self-Consciousness, perceptions arise experientially. And thoughts (or conceptual processes) also arise within the Intrinsically Self-Evident Current of Real Self-Consciousness—but thoughts arise only after (or on the basis of) the events and processes of experiential perception.

All perceptions (and, also, all the events of thinking) are entirely a reflected event, a Self-Mirrored and time-bound apparition, an illusion of separate "objectivity"—an illusion of not-Self. However, because all perceptions and all thoughts always arise dependently—and not only as a result of conditional causes, but entirely within the Always Senior Context of the Priorly Self-Evident and all-Mirroring Current of egoless Real Self-Consciousness—all perceptions, all thoughts, and, thus, <u>all</u> apparent "objects" <u>Are</u> modes (or merely apparent modifications) of the Perfectly Subjective (or Perfectly Non-"objective" and Non-"different") Current of Real Self-Consciousness <u>Itself</u>.

3.

Therefore, What Is Freedom?
Freedom Is Perfect (or Always Already Prior and Non-"different") Inherence in and As Reality Itself.

Freedom Is Perfect Fidelity to Truth Itself (Which Is Reality Itself).

Freedom Is to Always Already (or Priorly, or Intrinsically) Self-"Locate" (or Self-Identify) the Condition of the Real Self (or the Intrinsically Self-Evident and Inherently egoless Self-Condition That Is the Always Prior Context of all perception, all thought, all experience, all "objects", all "others", and all of apparent ego-"I", or seemingly separate self).

Freedom Is to Always Already Self-"Locate" (and, Thus, to Be) the Intrinsically Self-Evident and Inherently egoless Current of Feeling-Energy-Consciousness Itself—Always Already Prior to (and, yet, never separate from) perceptions, or thoughts, or "objects", or "others".

4.

On the basis of the Always Priorly (and always presently) Self-"Located" (and Inherently Indivisible, Non-separate, Non-"different", and egoless) Current of Feeling-Energy-Consciousness, all that (apparently, or experientially, and conditionally) arises "objectively" (as perceptions and thoughts) is Inherently (or Always Priorly) Transcended—without any act of dissociation, and without any act of seeking.

Therefore, all perceptions and all thoughts (or all "objects" of conditional experience) arise Acausally, Non-separately, and egolessly—Always Already Prior to any sense of "difference", necessity, dilemma, problem, or bondage.

Even the apparent ego-"I", and every apparent "other", and even all of conditionality and death, is Inherently (or Priorly, or Always Already) Transcended in the Intrinsically Self-Evident and Indivisible and Never-Broken Current (or Real-Self-Condition) of Inherently egoless Feeling-Energy-Consciousness—Which Is the Inherent Real Self (or Intrinsically Self-Evident Self-Condition) of all-and-All.

The apparent separation from any "other" (or from any "object" at all) is an experiential separation from (or apparent loss of) the conditionally apparent (or "objectified", or Self-Mirrored) "self" of separate ego-"I" (or "point of view").

Any perceived or conceived loss of the "objectified" (or Self-Mirrored) "self" (or any threat to the space-time "point of view" that is the separate ego-"I") tends to become "objectified" as reactivity (or merely <u>reactive</u> activity), in the form of fear, sorrow, or anger.

Any perception or conception of "objectified" and conditionally reactive "self" (or ego-"I") tends to become epitomized as the fear of death.

Therefore, Always Already Transcend the "objectified" and conditionally reactive (and entirely Self-Mirrored) ego-"self" (and all its "objects" and "others") in the Intrinsically Self-Evident Current of Inherently egoless Feeling-Energy-Consciousness (Which Is Reality Itself, or the Real-Condition Itself, Inherently Prior to "point of view" in space-time)—and, Thus and Thereby, Always Already Transcend death, and fear, and sorrow, and anger, too.

5.

Freedom Is Thus.
   Freedom Is the egoless Real Self-Condition—
   Wherein all perceptions, all thoughts, and all "objects"
are an Always Priorly Transcended (and, Thus, Perfectly
Forgotten) world-Mummery.
   Therefore, Peace Is Peace That Is Peace.
   Not-Two Is Peace.
   Not-Two Is Not Two.
   Not Two.
   Not-Two.
   Is Peace.
   Is-Peace.

LAST WORD

The Universal World-Prayer

A Prayer to
The Heart of Reality—
for Non-Sectarian Use
by All of Humankind

B eloved, <u>Inmost</u> Heart of <u>every</u> heart,
<u>do</u> <u>not</u> <u>Let</u> our human hearts be broken
by our merely mortal <u>suffering</u> here—
but <u>Make</u> our mortal human hearts break-<u>Free</u>
to an <u>unconditional</u> love of <u>You</u>,
that we may, <u>Thus</u>, love <u>all</u> living beings
with Love's <u>own</u> True, and <u>Truly</u> broken, Heart.■